Breaking Down
Barriers

Breaking Down Barriers

A Black Evangelical
Explains the Black Church

Dwight Perry

 Baker Books

A Division of Baker Book House Co
Grand Rapids, Michigan 49516

© 1998 by Dwight Perry

Published by Baker Books
a division of Baker Book House Company
P.O. Box 6287, Grand Rapids, MI 49516-6287

Printed in the United States of America

Library of Congress Cataloging-in-Publication Data

Perry, Dwight.
    Breaking down barriers : a Black Evangelical explains the
Black church / Dwight Perry.
        p.   cm.
    Includes bibliographical references.
    ISBN 0-8010-5709-4 (pbk.)
    1. Afro-Americans–Religion. 2. Evangelicalism–United States.
3. United States–Church history.   I. Title.
BR563.N4P46   1998
277.3'08'08996073–dc21   98-8102

For current information about all releases from Baker Book House, visit our web site:
http://www.bakerbooks.com

Contents

Separate and Unequal
The Black Church's Beginnings

The historical Black church is the result of the fusion of the best of African culture and the Christian faith. Such a fusion gave rise to what was probably one of the clearest expressions of New Testament Christianity America has ever seen,"[1] writes Dr. Tony Evans, renowned Black evangelical pastor, in his book *Are Blacks Spiritually Inferior to Whites?*

The entity at the heart of the Black community in America is the Black church. It has made its strong imprint not only on the Black community, but on the whole of society. Its modern-day form is a direct reflection of its African roots.

To understand the Black church of today, we must first study its beginnings in America. In this chapter we will build a foundation by examining the Black church's African roots, its organizational beginnings, and the way it became a separate and *un*equal entity. First, let's review how the Black church arose out of the pain of slavery.

From Slavery's Ashes

The Portuguese and the Spanish were the first Europeans to deal in the Black slave trade. They rationalized the enslavement of African people by asserting that it was God's way of bringing Black heathen into contact with Christianity, even if it meant a lifetime of enforced servitude. The institution of slavery was well-known in both southern Europe and Africa, but the rise of the European traffic in African slaves was the product of two cultural shifts in the fifteenth and sixteenth centuries that had taken place prior to the institution of slavery in the United States: the emergence of the national monarchies facing the Atlantic and the commercial revolution.

During the fifteenth and sixteenth centuries England and Spain took the lead in the expansion and colonization of the then-known world. Their competing governments sought to expand their power by conquering other territories, specifically those in Africa and later in the Americas. As they conquered, they exploited a territory's resources and stripped its land.

The new nations sought wealth and empire in Africa and in the New World. After Spain and Portugal had broken the commercial preeminence of the Italian city-states, Holland, France, and England successfully entered the contest for a share of the African trade and empires in the Americas.[2] As the economic boom in the Americas continued, cheap labor became an increasing necessity. To salve their conscience, the Europeans justified tearing people from their ancestral home in West Africa under the pretense of Christianizing them. This false premise for the slave trade later convinced many African Americans that Christianity was a religion of which they wanted no part.

No one knows the number of slaves transported to the new world. Some estimates are as high as twenty million;

more conservative estimates place the figure at fifteen million.[3] These men, women, boys, and girls were jammed into ships and transported from the Gulf of Guinea across the Atlantic to the New World in a trip called the middle passage. Millions never made it across the ocean, because the conditions aboard the ships were most inhumane.

Alexander Falconbridge, an eighteenth-century surgeon and eyewitness, described the squalid conditions this way:

> In favorable weather they are fed upon the deck, but in bad weather the food is given them below. Numerous quarrels take place among them, especially when they are put upon short allowance, which happened frequently if the passage from the coast of Guinea to the West India islands proves of unusual length. Exercise being deemed necessary for the preservation of their health, they are sometimes obliged to dance. If they go about it reluctantly, they are flogged. . . .
>
> The hardships and inconveniences suffered by the Negroes during the passage can scarcely be understood or conceived.
>
> The exclusion of fresh air was the most intolerable. For the purpose of bringing in fresh air, most of the ships had only five or six hatches that were closed during bad weather. The fresh air excluded thus, the cabin soon grew intolerably hot.
>
> The confined air, rendered noxious by the effluvia exhaled from the bodies and being repeatedly breathed, soon produced fevers and fluxes. The floors were covered with blood and mucus, which had proceeded from them in consequence of the flux, so much so it resembled a slaughter house.[4]

William Banks, in his book *The Black Church in the U.S.*, adds this description: "Shackled in irons, they huddled beneath the decks for sixteen hours at a time in unbearable heat, filth, and stench, barely surviving on stale, spoiled

9

food and stagnant water."[5] It was no wonder that many starved themselves to death.

The first Blacks to come to the United States were not slaves but indentured servants. They arrived in Jamestown, Virginia, in 1619. Indentured servitude, but not slavery, was allowed by English law. Indentured servants were bound temporarily and could be sold for apprenticeship or because of vagrancy. However, it was not long in America before Blacks were legally bought and sold as slaves for life. By 1787 there were nearly seven hundred thousand Negro slaves in the United States and about fifty-nine thousand free Blacks.

Eli Whitney's invention of the cotton gin in 1793 greatly enhanced the South's economy. This simple device for separating the seeds from the cotton fiber made production of cotton faster than it had been and much more profitable. Cotton became the staple crop, the "king," of the South, and the demand for cotton raised the demand for slave labor to unparalleled levels. By the mid-1800s nearly three quarters of the slaves were involved in cotton agriculture.

As slavery moved west, the conditions of the slave deteriorated at an alarming rate. By this time society considered slaves no more than property with no rights and not even an opportunity to be legally married. I am old enough to remember stories told by those who were only one generation away from slavery. These stories of horror left an indelible impression on me.

Slaves lived on plantations, typically in crude, drafty, leaky clapboard shacks without furniture and often in overcrowded filth. The conditions of slavery promoted family instability and promiscuity. Slave traders would rip apart families arriving in the United States. Murder, rape, and inhumane punishment became the norm for treatment of Negro slaves. Inbreeding between White men and slave women was a daily occurrence.

Out of this context of misery, oppression, and pain, the invisible Black church emerged in the early to mid-1700s.

African Roots

Contrary to stereotypes, the "slave was not a backward, savage person who had no perception of the true God. He was already acclimated to God. Yet, as can be said of all cultures, the African recognized God through 'His invisible attributes' (Rom. 1:20)."[6] A. H. Fauset said, "It is safe to assume that not one Negro in the original cargo of slaves . . . was a member of the Christian faith." However, there is some evidence that they were baptized Christians who either were traded or pirated and transferred from a Spanish war vessel to a Dutch frigate.[7]

There is disagreement, however, on whether the Black church as an institution came to America with its roots tied to Africa. Historian E. Franklin Frazier argued in his classic book *The Negro Church in America* that establishing continuity between African religious practices and the Negro church in America was impossible. He said the crisis of slavery was too great to sustain any remnant of African heritage and that the successful extinction by slave owners of the native African languages meant that religious concepts that could not be easily expressed in English would have been quickly lost.[8]

Others disagree with this assessment. Scholar W. E. B. Du Bois has defended his belief that the Black church is the only African institution that came to America with the slaves.[9] Historic facts seem to support this theory. The customs of the African religious practice created a context where belief in a supernatural being already was an acceptable conclusion. Some of the practices—the elevation of the African priest as community leader, the reliance on oral communication, the significance of developing worshiping communities of faith—laid the groundwork for accepting Christianity.

Henry Mitchell in his work *Black Belief* says contemporary Black religion is not only what you saw in Africa historically, but is an accurate reflection of the religion practiced today in Africa. "Thus, to think of the Black church as a variant form of white missionary enterprise is fallacious. Rather, the essentials were already present; what Europeans provided was simply affixed to an already existent theological and social structure."[10]

Melville Herskovits has this to say concerning the influence of the African past on the slaves' religious belief systems:

> The prominent place held by religion in the life of the Negro in the United States, and the special forms assumed by Negro versions of Christian dogma and ritual, are customarily explained as compensatory devices to meet the social and economic frustration experienced by Negroes during slavery and after emancipation. Such explanations have the partial validity we have already seen them to hold for various phases of black secular life; but, as must be emphasized again, cannot be regarded as telling the entire causal tale. For underlying the life of the American black is a deep religious bent that is but the manifestation here of a similar drive that everywhere in black societies makes the supernatural a major focus of interest.[11]

Herskovits also writes about the supernaturalism prevalent among Africans.

> The river spirits were among the most powerful of those inhabiting the supernatural world, and the priests of this cult were among the most powerful members of tribal priestly groups. . . . In all parts of the new world where African religious beliefs have persisted, moreover, the river cult, or in broader terms the cult of water spirits, holds an important place. All this testifies to the vitality of this element in African religion and supports the conclusion as to the possible influence such priests wielded even as slaves.[12]

12

Modes of Values Transmission

Many African Americans today have been influenced not only theologically but also sociologically by the White training systems to which they have been exposed. Therefore, we may have difficulty grasping not only the significance of Mitchell's conclusions but also their validity. Before we can appreciate the slaves' spiritual presuppositions, then, we must come to grips with the process by which the transmission of these values took place.

In an introductory anthropology class one of the basic premises taught is the fact that when people transfer from one place to another (whether voluntarily or involuntarily) they take with them a part of their culture. For example, one hundred years ago many Europeans migrated to the United States, and today we can still see the cultural residue of that migration when we visit Greektowns or Germantowns in many American cities.

This phenomenon is even more consistently visible when the relocation into another culture is by force rather than by choice. One of the episodes in the Bible that most graphically illustrates this point is the Jewish enslavement in Egypt. One of the keys to the Jewish survival was their relentless faith in Yahweh and their undying desire to secure for themselves the land God had promised Abraham. Although Moses, the Israelite baby that Pharaoh's daughter rescued in the bulrushes, was raised in Pharaoh's household (and nursed by the mother who had given him up to save his life), he reverted to the faith of his birth.

Tony Evans explains this in his book *Are Blacks Spiritually Inferior to Whites?*

> When people take their cultures with them to a new locale, it is the central elements of the culture that are the easiest to salvage. The centerpiece of the west African culture was God. All of life was interpreted in terms of the Divine. This explains why there was such a quick and easy gravitation to-

ward Christianity. . . . Since God was the African slave's reference point for all of life, He would be the first one to whom the slave would appeal, particularly in a time of crisis.[13]

Three foundational characteristics[14] of the Black church today seem to have a direct tie to its African roots:

> *Strong reliance on oral communication.* The African priest was the transmitter of the values and the history of one generation to the next. His role as history bearer created a strong reliance on his ability to relate orally his people's history and culture. Even after leaving Africa, the elder of the clan took on this role. Eventually the Black preacher assumed the role in the community.
>
> *The tendency toward orthodoxy and a high view of God.* Blacks historically have represented one of the true anomalies in American society. Many are staunchly conservative from a religious point of view, while liberal politically and socially. This conservative theological position is evident in the way the Black church views such issues as the role of women in leadership or the church's primary theological teachings. Women, the primary church workers, have been excluded from the role of senior pastor in local congregations. (Even in the Pentecostal wing, this is true for the most part.) Theologically the Black church fairly consistently holds to the cardinal doctrines of inerrancy, the virgin birth, and the lordship of Christ. The tendency today of Black churches to deviate from the center is a result of interaction with mainline White Protestant denominations.
>
> *A strong connection between theology and life.* While many White evangelicals and fundamentalists have erroneously divided the spiritual dimensions of the gospel from its social dimensions, within the Black church, one's theology is not given credence unless it includes a social dimension.

The modus operandi of the tribes in Africa was oral recitation. Common in this way of transference of values was the tendency toward a high view of God and a strong connection between theology and one's daily life. These roots carry through in today's Black church in America, where preaching is supreme, orthodoxy is affirmed, and adoration of Jehovah God is expressed in a mystical manner, reminiscent of generations-old tribal communication.

Despite the degradation Blacks have experienced in America, they preserved a sense of reality by maintaining their identity through the affirmation of and reflection on their African past and its values. These values were passed on to succeeding generations through the means African Americans knew best—their strong oral tradition. Initially the primary place of transmission for these values was the secret worshiping community. The slave—at the risk of death—used secret songs to communicate in code, without the master being privy to the message.

Early Christian Outreach to Blacks

When slaves were first brought to America, Christian churches were hesitant to evangelize them because they feared that if the Africans became Christians, this would, of necessity, alter their status as slaves. Various legal rulings, however, provided protection to the slave owner. It was affirmed that conversion to Christianity was not incongruous with a slave's status. Thus Christian denominations began to freely evangelize the slaves.

The Anglican Society of the Propagation of the Gospel in Foreign Parts, founded in 1701, was the first Protestant group organized to evangelize Blacks.[15] They had little success, however, partly because of their ritualistic form of worship and partly because of their racist attitudes. Anglicans were large slaveholders on the Atlantic coast, and the church would not allow their one Black church—St.

15

Thomas in Philadelphia—to participate in the denomination's deliberations. Even today, Black membership in the Anglican or Episcopal church remains relatively small.

Most of the denominations, such as Quakers, Congregationalists, and Presbyterians, that made a concerted effort to evangelize Blacks did so in the North, so they did not have a wide influence among the slaves. The Great Awakening was far more effective in its evangelistic efforts. The preaching ministry of Jonathan Edwards in 1734 and 1735 attracted large numbers of Blacks to Christianity. The Methodists and Baptists experienced tremendous growth due to their emphasis on reaching out to the common man. Soon more Africans began embracing Christianity. The acknowledgment of the existence of a supreme being by most African cultures made it relatively easy for the African slave to replace his or her concept of a divine being with the Jehovah God of Scripture.

Slaves began attending their master's church, although they were restricted to sitting in the back rows and could hold no leadership role. Some congregations even erected dividers several feet high so Blacks were not physically mingling with the White congregants. But many slaves continued to worship on their own. The secret meetings of the earlier slave days were still going on.

Separate and Unequal

Most converted slaves worshiped in their master's church, but there existed two other types of church for the Christian slave: separate Black churches under White leadership and supervision; separate Black churches with Black leadership. The latter began to increase in number as sentiment grew among Blacks for separation from this system of inferiority.

In the pre–Revolutionary War period most Blacks who were not part of their master's church attended Black churches under White leadership. Whites believed that Blacks could not be trusted to meet separately because of the ignorance of Blacks and their heathen tendencies. More germane, however, was the White slave master's fear that meeting without White supervision would empower the Negro slave to create dissension and organize rebellion.

It is true that from the end of the 1700s through the Civil War, the Black church's leaders, such as Harriet Tubman and Sojourner Truth, were staunch supporters of the Underground Railroad and freedom for Blacks. Nat Turner was a slave preacher who believed he was directed by God to attempt a violent overthrow of slavery in 1831. In fact even in more recent history Black church leaders have been firmly behind civil rights reformers. Civil rights movements not only had their foundation in the Black church in the 1950s and 1960s, but the Black church continues to strongly support efforts that pursue equality.

The movement toward separation of Blacks from their master's church began because the increasing number of Black worshipers felt deeply their status as unwanted outsiders in the White congregations. The first Black church established in America was founded between 1773 and 1775, in Silver Bluff, South Carolina, by a White preacher named Palmer. George Liele, a slave freed by his master when he became a preacher, pastored this church.

After the Revolutionary War, Blacks made determined efforts for independence of worship and, as a result, other churches sprang up: in 1776 the Harrison Street Baptist Church in Richmond, Virginia; in 1790 the First African Baptist Church of Lexington, Kentucky; and in 1809 the Abyssinian Baptist Church of New York. At first, free Blacks were responsible for these independent assemblies, especially in the North. But there were churches in the South that were established and pastored by slaves.

The man most historians credit as the father of Black denominations in America is Richard Allen. Allen was a slave who was able to buy his freedom in 1777. He had been converted to Christianity that same year, under Methodist preaching, and quickly established himself as a preacher. He was allowed to travel with White preachers for the purpose of spreading the gospel, often visiting New Jersey and Philadelphia. In Philadelphia in 1787 he established the Free African Society with Absalom Jones, another Black preacher. The society was formed as a mutual aid society but it became the basis of the first Black church when Allen, Jones, and others were poorly treated in the White St. George Methodist Episcopal Church. When Jones was pulled from his knees during prayer because he, Allen, and others were in the "wrong" section of the church, they all walked out.

It was then that the Free African Society began conducting its own religious services and in 1794 Bethel Church was founded. Allen insisted that the church be Methodist in orientation, since he believed the "plain and simple gospel" of Methodism met the need of Blacks better than did the Episcopal service.

Early the influence of Black America's African roots became evident in the church. Many of the churches incorporated the word *African* into their names. The specific emotive style of worship emerged, taken from the worship patterns of the tribes. These churches also placed strong emphasis on oral rather than written communication, a fact that elevated the preacher (one could not be a preacher unless one could *really* preach) to a platform similar to that of the tribal chieftain, whose influence over the daily affairs of his tribe (in the pastor's case, over his parishioners) was monumental.

Another indication of cultural transference was the communal character of the church. Coming from a tribal/clan background, the slave was dependent on his communal environment for survival but when he arrived in America, most family connections were severed. The church became the surrogate family that provided a place of connectedness. This communal nature of the church became its key strength.

Five Factors Converge

Author Tony Evans has identified five factors that converged to birth the Black church.[16]

1. *The reality of slavery forced the slave to look within himself for meaning.* When the slaves arrived in America, they had nowhere to turn in the face of the traumatic upheaval of their lives, except inward. By relying on what they had been taught, they were able to retain their history, their culture, and their religious heritage. There they found "the most significant aspect of their past life in Africa: God!"

   "Such a realization of the necessity for faith in the centrality of God resulted in the prioritization of the spiritual dimensions of life" and attracted them to Christianity.

2. *White organizations became more aggressive in evangelizing Blacks.* Although initially they had no interest in evangelizing Blacks, a few White denominations (such as the Baptists and Methodists) became more aggressive as a result of the Great Awakening in 1726 and the revivalist preaching of Jonathan Edwards and George Whitfield, who traveled in all the colonies between 1738 and 1769, heightening the moral tone of the people. Many of the revivals were "full of emotion, shouting, dancing, and other verbal expressions. This reminded the slaves of their own worship experiences and helped to make Christianity palatable to them."

3. *Slaves began integrating their African beliefs with what they were hearing concerning this new Christian faith.* They heard the gospel not only from the perspective of one's need for personal salvation and forgiveness of sin, but also as the voice of hope and liberation. Since community was deeply ingrained in the typical slave's experience, the community's reinforcement of the Christian faith caused slaves to embrace the Christian worldview as their own.

4. *The Bible was the first book to which they were exposed.* This exposure gave them more hope, as they began to see how God was the God of the oppressed and how he had and would continue to deliver his people.

5. *The Black preacher provided the link between Africa and America.* The African people were accustomed to focusing on the priest as religious and community leader. This laid the foundation for the development of the Black church and the rise of the Black preacher. We will examine this phenomenon in more detail in chapter 5.

A Foundation for the Future

A dichotomy between faith and practice never developed within the context of the Black church, because the church played a central role in the freedom of its people from the degradation of slavery. The Black church *had* to develop a holistic perspective on what the gospel means to everyday life to help its members cope with the anathema of being Black in White America.

The White church in this country developed in the absence of oppression; it could afford to dichotomize the gospel, allowing it to apply to spiritual issues but not social ones. By contrast, slavery caused the Black church to develop a theology that was not only more holistic in its application but that stressed such themes as liberation both here and in the afterlife and created a theology of hope centered on heaven that was central to the gospel message. Additionally, its emotive form of worship reinforced experiential rather than didactic tendencies.

The reliance on a strong oral tradition provided the impetus for the development of the Black preacher—in essence the new African priest—to become the predominate figure in the Black community. Only within the last fifteen to twenty years has this changed with the Black preacher's centrality being replaced by sports, business, and entertainment personalities.

Essentially the Black church's existence is a result of God's people failing to apply correctly God's Word to their lives. In Ephesians 2:13–20 Paul reminds us that we are one in Christ and that Christ has broken down the dividing wall of hostility between people. Yet on the prevailing cultural foundations, the Black church in America developed an identity that has been carried through to the modern day. We will examine each of its foundational differences from the White church more fully in the coming chapters.

— 2 —

The Only Game in Town

The Role of the Black Church in the Post-Slavery Community

Lerone Bennett in his book *Before the Mayflower* describes the post-slavery Reconstructionist period:

Never before had the sun shone so bright.

A former slave named Blanche Keso Bruce was representing Mississippi in the United States Senate. Pickney Benton Pinchback, young, charming, daring, was sitting in the governor's office in Louisiana.

In Mississippi, South Carolina and Louisiana, black lieutenant governors were sitting on the right hand of power. A black was secretary of state in Florida; a black was on the state supreme court in South Carolina. In these and other Southern states, blacks were superintendents of education, state treasurers, adjutant generals, solicitors, judges and major generals of militia. Robert H. Wood was mayor of Natchez, Mississippi, and Norris Wright Cuney was running for mayor of Galveston, Texas. Seven blacks were sitting in the House of Representatives.

Nor was this all. Blacks and whites were going to school together, riding on streetcars together and cohabiting, in and out of wedlock. An interracial board was running the University of South Carolina, where a black professor, Richard T. Greener, was teaching white and black youth metaphysics and logic. . . .

The millennium hadn't come, of course, but there were some who believed it was around the next turning. . . .

These things, improbable as they may seem now, happened in America during the ten improbable years (1867–77) of Black Reconstruction.[1]

Reconstruction was a unique period in American history, especially in the life and history of African Americans. Thrust on us as quickly as the Emancipation Proclamation of 1861 had given us our freedom, it was truly an era that for many Blacks almost approached the biblical prophecy of a new millennium. For the first time in the history of the country, Blacks held a certain degree of power. The South was being rebuilt, and it appeared at least at the onset that African Americans would play a major role in its redevelopment.

W. E. B. Du Bois called them the "mystic years." Intoxicated perhaps by the emotional bang of the big war, taunted by the arrogance of the conquered South, and spurred on by economic and political factors, the North took in these years the longest strides America has ever taken: it decided to try democracy.[2]

At the conclusion of the Civil War, Blacks found themselves free men for the first time since their arrival on America's shores. They were even called "freedmen," symbolizing their new relationship, not only with their former slave masters, but to American society. The question that still needed to be addressed was, "Freed to what?" Not only did they not have a place to go—having been released from their former masters—but they did not have the skills, income, or land to build a new life.

Blacks for more than 150 years had been entrapped by the bonds of slavery. But although these bonds were excruciating, they, nevertheless, gave African Americans a well-defined context out of which to operate. This context, despite its pain, created a certain degree of normalcy and predictability as an entire race of people became conditioned to existing within this oppressive, exploitative social structure. Not having this context as his frame of reference caused the Black man to experience a certain degree of disequilibrium as well as insecurity as to what to do next and how to begin to assimilate into the mainstream of American society.

Congress approved a temporary solution on March 3, 1865, by creating the Freedmen's Bureau. The Freedmen's Bureau, according to historian Lerone Bennett, was "the first federal welfare agency. During its lamentably short life (1865–72), the bureau was an Urban League, WPA, CIO and War on Poverty all wrapped up into a prototypical NAACP." He continues,

> It stood between the freedmen and the wrath of their former slavemasters. It gave direct medical aid to some one million freedmen, established hospitals and social agencies and distributed over twenty-one million rations, many of them to poverty-stricken whites. The agency also established day schools, night schools, industrial schools, institutes and colleges. Many of the major black colleges were founded or received substantial financial aid from the Freedmen's Bureau.[3]

Despite its aura of imminent relief for the newly freed African Americans, the Freedmen's Bureau failed miserably. It was marked with inefficiencies, corruption, inadequate financial backing, and resistance on every turn by those still committed to the institution of slavery. The Bureau also did not address the long-term needs of the former slave—those of property ownership and economic equity and reform. Thus the major structural impact on society and on the conditions of the Black man that had been predicted never materialized. The Freedmen's Bureau did, however, provide temporary relief for the thousands of former slaves who were literal nomads, with no place to call home, in the great country that had been built through their labor and the labor of their forefathers.

A New Bondage—Sharecropping

Western societies tend to place the issue of economics above politics. This was true of the radical Reconstruction period. Although they tried to deal with the gross inequalities between the races through sweeping political reforms, which would not be surpassed until the civil rights era a century later, reformers of the period failed to grapple with the economic realities that slavery, and its replacement system—sharecropping—were based on economic issues. Sharecropping tied former slaves to an economic system that continued to exploit them for the former masters' gain.

Thaddeus Stevens, a Reconstructionalist, originated the phrase, "forty acres and a mule."

> In and out of Congress, the indomitable old Pennsylvanian demanded that large plantations be broken up and distributed to the freedmen in forty-acre lots. "We have turned, or are about to turn, loose four million slaves without a hut to shelter them or a cent in their pockets," he said. "The infernal laws of slavery have prevented them from acquiring an education, understanding the common laws of contract, or of managing the ordinary business of life. This Congress is bound to provide for them until they can take care of themselves. If we do not furnish them with homesteads, and hedge them around with protective laws;

if we leave them to the legislation of their late masters, we had better have left them in bondage."[4]

What resulted from Stevens's passionate rhetoric was an economic system—sharecropping—that I have come to call the new slavery. It was a form of continued manipulation and domination by the White majority community under the guise of a decent way to earn a living that was politically acceptable and perfectly legal under the law of the land. It became an exceptionally exploitative system because it gave the newly freed slave an illusion of independence and autonomy. This system, however good it looked on the outside to the former slave, became a ball and chain around the Black man or woman's neck.

The sharecropping system allowed the freedman to rent from the plantation owner a plot of land on which he could raise a crop, promising to give a certain proportion of the crop as payment toward the purchase of the land. Usually, however, the freedman was never able to buy the land and he never achieved the autonomy and genuine economic freedom he sought. This was because of the unscrupulous practices of the plantation owners who arbitrarily assessed fees on supposedly unpaid bills and charged exorbitant interest rates to keep the sharecropper in constant economic bondage.

Planters generally would have preferred a system whereby Blacks contracted by the year to work for specified wages, but the shortage of available cash right after the war encouraged them to adopt a plan whereby they shared the crop with the black workers. A number of scholars hold that the freedmen themselves were largely responsible for the development of sharecropping, because they regarded the contract labor system, under which they worked in labor gangs, as too reminiscent of slavery times. Renting was desirable, even under a sharecropping rather than a cash arrangement, because tenants could organize their own time and be more independent than a hired laborer.[5]

Because the sharecroppers did not own the land and were not schooled in accounting, plantation owners charged them exorbitant prices for goods at the plantation stores, being certain they bought on credit—borrowing against their crops at outrageous interest rates. Without adequate education, they had to depend on the planter's version of the accounts. "After the crop was sold, they were likely to end up in debt to the planter, particularly in a poor year. Out of this arose the system of debt peonage, whereby insolvent croppers, unable to repay debts from one year to another, were required by law to work indefinitely for the same unscrupulous planter."[6]

Quoting Bennett again, "The land problem was linked to the larger problems of the South and the status of blacks. Nothing could be done with the conquered South until the status of blacks was settled. The reverse was also true. Nothing could be done for blacks until the status of the conquered South was settled."[7]

Neither President Lincoln nor his successor, President Johnson, did much to improve the condition of the former slaves. Not only was there no adequate provision made for their physical and economic needs, but their legal rights were left unprotected as well.

It is unfortunate that only a limited attempt to truly consider the rights and needs of African Americans was made in the South and also in the North, which was supposed to be the defender of the African American's rights. "Throughout this period, and on into the 1870s, hundreds of freedmen were massacred in 'riots' staged and directed by policemen and other government officials."[8] And in random attacks people throughout the South terrorized unarmed Blacks. Finally, however, the national mood began to change, giving Charles Sumner and Stevens the impetus to wrest control of the Reconstruction from President Johnson and push "through the Fourteenth and Fifteenth amendments and enabling legislation which sent troops into the South to protect the rights of blacks."[9]

Blacks throughout the South began to feel enfranchised. They became involved in the political process in record numbers. White southerners became increasingly frustrated. They saw not only their old South taken away from them and occupied by the North, but their former slaves rise to positions of authority over them.

So White southerners manufactured the myths that Blacks were inept and corrupt and portrayed Blacks as buffoons controlled by the northern carpetbaggers and the southern scalawags. Most Blacks who embraced the political process did so with enthusiasm and insight. But the subtle and subversive attack on Black leadership laid the foundation for the radical, sustained assault on Black political leaders that continues today.

> One by one, the local leaders were killed, driven out of the state or compromised. In Mississippi, to cite only one case, Charles Caldwell, the courageous state senator, was killed in broad daylight and his body was "grotesquely turned completely over by the impact of innumerable shots fired at close range." Nobody knows how many Charles Caldwells died in this period. But conservative estimates run into the thousands.[10]
>
> By 1874 only four states—South Carolina, Florida, Louisiana, and Mississippi—were still in the Republican column. In these states black voters were so deeply entrenched that nothing short of a revolution could dislodge them. Southern Democrats did not shrink from the task. "ORGANIZE! ORGANIZE! ORGANIZE!" said a bold headline in the *Charleston News and Observer*. "We must render this a white man's government," another newspaper said, "or convert the land into a Negro man's cemetery." . . .
>
> Newspapers which had been indifferent to or amused by the antics of black politicians turned mean. Now all black

29

politicians were devils: "the shameless, heartless, vile, grasping, deceitful, creeping . . . pirates." . . .

While this propaganda campaign was going on, the white population organized for war and systematically disarmed the black population.[11]

They searched the homes of Blacks and took away their arms. Playing on the fears of a race war, "Democrats succeeded in disarming or emasculating the predominately black state militia."[12] Polls were closed on election days. The optimism that had ushered in the Reconstruction era soon disintegrated into alienation of the Black man.

Public opinion in the North was beginning to change. It was impossible for Reconstruction to succeed without a strong federal presence in the South. This prevailed in the initial years because the interests of the conservative White Republicans—national unity, supremacy of northern fiscal policy, and high tariffs—paralleled the interests of Blacks. However, politics shifted back to business as usual when southern Whites began to regain economic and political power.

For almost eighty years after the end of Reconstruction, the biases of slavery made themselves known in the form of Jim Crowism. *Jim Crow* is a slang term that describes the post-Reconstruction practice of systematically segregating and suppressing Blacks. The term came from a pitiful character played by Thomas Rice, a White minstrel performer. It came to be used as a description of the Negro, crippled by segregationist laws.

Too Good to Be True

The South had had an opportunity to see the reality of a society where, as Dr. Martin Luther King Jr. said years later that "hundreds hence would be judged not so much on the color of their skin but the content of their character."[13] The Civil Rights Act of 1867 had brought to the Black man the right to vote. The Reconstruction Act of 1867 had provided that each southern state was to be placed under a military governor until a convention, chosen on the basis of universal manhood suffrage, wrote a constitution that would meet the requirements set by Congress. The Fifteenth Amendment proposed by Congress in 1869 and ratified the following year had reinforced the Reconstruction Act and the new southern state constitutions. It had also secured the vote for Blacks in those northern states where they had been disfranchised because these states in the North had failed to ratify the Thirteenth Amendment.

For the first time in the history of this country Blacks had been able to hold public office. They had occupied governmental positions at all levels, including the U.S. Senate. Fourteen Blacks had sat in the House of Representatives. The highest state official had been lieutenant governor. It had appeared that this new South would be characterized by equality for all.

Unfortunately the gains Blacks seemed to make during the Reconstruction period were nothing more than a mirage. With the infamous Compromise of 1877, when Rutherford B. Hayes agreed to the removal of federal troops from the South in exchange for southern electoral votes in a deadlocked presidential contest, the Reconstruction ended. With the end of the Reconstruction period, nearly eighty years of disfranchisement of African Americans in the South began.

Within the next twenty years, life for African Americans in the South became as oppressive as it was under slavery. Jim Crow policies were literally ratified and legitimated by the highest court in the land through the doctrine of separate but equal laid down in the *Plessy v. Ferguson* decision of 1896.

With the removal of the federal troops, the constraints that had kept southern Whites somewhat at bay were gone.

31

This brought about unrestrained Ku Klux Klan violence, as well as economic discrimination and the electoral obstacles of poll taxes and frivolous registration procedures, such as the grandfather clause that stated, "If a man or his ancestors voted on or before a selected date [a date on which there were no Black voters] he could vote and escape the other provisions." Black codes that had been instituted soon after the Civil War helped maintain the atmosphere of oppression. The codes were

> a system of social control that would be substituted for slavery, fix the Negro in a subordinate place in the social order, and provide a manageable and inexpensive labor force. Blacks who were unemployed or without a permanent residence were declared vagrants. They could be arrested and fined and if unable to pay, be bound out for terms of labor. States enacted careful provisions governing contracts between employer and laborer—in several states the words "master" and "servant" were freely used. . . . Stiff penalties were provided for those who did not fulfill these contracts or who encouraged blacks to evade them. These statutes generally guaranteed Negros the right to sue and be sued and to own property, but they ordinarily could not bear firearms, could testify only in cases involving blacks, and in Mississippi could own only certain types of property.[14]

In the *Plessy v. Ferguson* case the Supreme Court said

> state laws requiring "separate but equal" accommodations for blacks were a "reasonable" use of state police powers, adding: "The object of the [Fourteenth] Amendment was undoubtedly to enforce the absolute equality of the two races before the law, but in the nature of things it could not have been intended to abolish distinctions based on color, or to enforce social, as distinguished from political equality, or a commingling of the two races upon terms unsatisfactory to either."

Justice John Marshall Harlan was prophetic in dissent. Laws requiring segregation, he said, fostered ideas of caste and inferiority and would lead to additional aggression against blacks. For "in view of the Constitution, in the eye of the law, there is in this country no superior, dominant, ruling class of citizens. There is no caste here. Our Constitution is color-blind, and neither knows nor tolerates classes among citizens. . . . It is, therefore, to be regretted that this high tribunal, the final expositor of the fundamental law of the land, has reached the conclusion that it is competent for a state to regulate the enjoyment by citizens of their civil rights solely upon the basis of race. In my opinion, the judgment this day rendered will, in time, prove to be quite as pernicious as the decision made by this tribunal in the Dred Scott case.[15]

After the *Plessy v. Ferguson* decision, the South became even more aggressive in the implementation of what was in actuality a quasi-slavery system. Lynchings, Jim Crow laws, and the total disfranchisement of Black people had escalated by the turn of the century, becoming an accepted way of life in America for the next sixty years.

Where Was the Church?

Despite the economic, political, and social upheaval, the Black church flourished during the period following the Civil War through the end of the nineteenth century. It became the center of the Black community; the predominant venue of self-expression, recognition, and shelter from a cruel, hostile White world; and the only institution Blacks could control.

Two phenomena occurred during this period that would have long-term, substantive impact on the rise of the Black church to the place of prominence it would hold for more than one hundred years after the Civil War:

- The formerly invisible slave church (of the southern plantation days) emerged, becoming not only visible but vibrant.

33

- Free Negroes, especially those who had been free prior to the Emancipation Proclamation, began to assert themselves and pull out of White movements and churches they felt maintained a superior-to-inferior relationship with them.

Jumping Forward in Time

"Run Jesse Run" "If not now, when? If not Jesse, who?" "Now is the time!"

In political revival meetings and voter registration drives in black communities across the country during the summer and fall of 1983, thousands of ordinary black folk chanted for their favorite preacher-politician to enter the presidential contest. Rev. Jesse Jackson's controversial candidacy in the 1984 and 1988 presidential primaries for the Democratic Party is to be understood in the context of black religious history in the United States. Too often scholars and journalists have sharply demarcated religion and politics into separate spheres, thereby misunderstanding much that has happened in black history and the continuing role of the Black Church. As Manning Marable has pointed out: "The majority of Black theologians and sociologists of religion tend to make a radical separation between Black faith and the specific political praxis of Black clergy. Most political science research on the Civil Rights Movement concentrates on King's role as a centrist within the broad and often fractious united front that constituted the desegregationist campaign, and ignores the historical relationship between Black politics and faith. Few historians have seriously explored the Movement's impact on the evolution of the Black Church."[16]

One need look only at the last twenty years to understand the implications of that statement. Not only is it true that most Black political leaders have come right out of the church, but it is the church that still has the ability to politically galvanize the African American community. This phenomenon reinforces the reality of the Black political experience here in America—religion has been a central component. There are several factors that have contributed to this reality:

1. Prior to and during the Atlantic slave trade, the traditional worldview and customs of the Africans were permeated by religion, with no division between the sacred and secular. African kings and queens governed all aspects of life, including religion.
2. Whites were ambivalent about the conversion of slaves to Christianity. This resulted in slaves being converted and establishing the Black church, the only institution in our society that was controlled by Blacks.
3. The Black church played an important role in helping Blacks survive slavery.
4. The Black church has consistently been the one viable entity in the Black community that is involved in a multitude of community-based issues.[17]

Black Community Institutions

One reaction to the discrimination and segregation imposed by Whites in the late eighteenth and early nineteenth centuries was the formation of Black fraternal organizations. These organizations not only provided economic help for African Americans, but became a source of political power and influence within the Black community.

As leaders in the community, the church ministers naturally played an important role in all African American affairs and were involved with the mutual aid organizations that assisted members in times of distress; recorded births, marriages, and deaths; and provided burials. The first known mutual aid society was that founded by Richard Allen and Absalom Jones in 1787—the Free African Society (see chapter 1). This organization was typical of those that would follow. Its members ministered to the local community, pooling resources for mutual support, and they helped make possible Black cultural advancement.

These societies quickly multiplied throughout the northern cities. By the 1830s there were one hundred organizations, averaging seventy-five members each, in Philadelphia alone. Mutual aid societies also existed in the South, although their activities were limited after White fears of slave insurrections resulted in laws curtailing the assembly of Negroes. Baltimore had the largest number of benevolent societies. By 1835 there were more than thirty, with membership ranging from 35 to 150.

Similar to mutual aid societies in their purpose were the secret fraternal orders, such as Masons and Odd Fellows. With rituals, ceremonies, and regalia, they gave members prestige and performed economic functions similar to those of the mutual aid societies. My father, a product of the Deep South, took great pride in his membership in the Masons. Blacks were excluded from the secret orders organized by Whites, so the Masons and the Odd Fellows that were organized by Blacks obtained their charters directly from England. The lodge provided Blacks a sense of solidarity and community involvement. Along with the church and mutual aid society, the lodge provided an essential vehicle for networking.

Later these societies would work with the church to take the lead in eradicating segregation and inequalities.

Economics

During the post–Civil War period, there was a tremendous need to raise the economic status of the Black man. Freed from slavery, he found himself condemned to a life of poverty. He owned little and was at the bottom of American society.

The Freedman's Savings and Trust Company had been chartered in 1865 and held the meager savings of many newly emancipated African Americans as well as monies of benevolent associations and churches. The bank collapsed in 1874, sending many African Americans into a crisis of distrust of all banking institutions. It was at this point in history that churches, secret societies, and mutual aid organizations began creating their own financial institutions. Insurance companies, funeral parlors, and mortuaries soon followed.

In 1887 there was not a single black-owned bank but by 1908 fifty-five banks had been started and forty-seven were in operation.

Toward the end of the nineteenth and at the beginning of the twentieth century the first black insurance companies began to appear, developing from the financial resources of both the mutual aid and burial societies and the fraternal orders. . . .

The fraternal orders were the primary mobilizers of black finance but the churches ranked second. Clergymen often played a prominent role in organizing insurance societies and banks.[18]

Moral and Educational Foundations

Black churches, mutual aid societies, and fraternal lodges were attempts at creating moral communities that would spread the ethos of economic uplift and self-help. Not only was the Black church integral to the political and economic development of Black people, but it also was integral to the development of effective systems of education that were used in the Black community.

No other area of black life received a higher priority from black churches than education. Despite the fact that teaching a slave to read and write was illegal during slavery, one of the most persistent desires of the slaves was to be educated. First of all, literacy was the key to the scriptures, the Word of God, but education was also a rebuttal of the prevailing allegation that black people were a different order of human being, incapable of learning and manipulating the master's language. For many slaves education was tied to their religion, a coveted doorway to the faith and its promises. . . . After emancipation, the newly freed people of all ages swamped the schools.[19]

Many of these schools were church-based. With the aid of the American Mission Society and the Freedmen's Bureau, many schools were established—elementary, secondary, and post-secondary. Some of the more prestigious Black colleges—Morehouse, Spelman, and Tuskegee—began in church basements. Whole denominations saw the need to create colleges and seminaries to equip prospective ministers.

Today the Black church continues to be one of the leading institutions in the Black community in terms of its impact politically, economically, and educationally. There has been a renewed sense, especially in communities of poverty, of the need of church-based community economic development systems that are able to marshal workers and develop indigenous community resources.

—3—

From Plantation to Ghetto
Finding a New Home in a Strange Land

The period following the Great Compromise of 1877, when Reconstruction came to an end, was a time when Blacks lost ground. The Emancipation Proclamation had set Blacks free. People like Thaddeus Stevens had laid the foundation for the radical Reconstruction of the South in which Blacks held significant places of power. Then in a flash, progress toward real freedom came to a halt. Blacks became increasingly the victims of discrimination, proscription, and mob violence. This was particularly true in the South, where the withdrawal of federal troops and the acceptance of the White democratic debauchery of the Black man left the southern Black defenseless. The result was the unimpeded development of a race system (Jim Crowism) that was in essence institutional slavery without some of the political and economic ramifications.

As a people, Blacks were in a state of crisis. They were living in a world that sought to exclude them from participation in the so-called freedoms they allegedly had received. Though free, they still lived like slaves in continual fear for their lives under intense racial oppression.

The freedoms for which so many had given their lives, including the right to influence the political process through voting, were being taken away—one by one. Whether through election fraud, violence, or intrusions on his personal integrity, from the latter half of the nineteenth century through the first half of the twentieth century, the Black man experienced unparalleled pain.

"Mississippi in 1890 and South Carolina in 1895 were the first states to amend their constitutions to virtually disfranchise practically all Negros." These constitutions had loopholes that a racist judge could apply with little accountability. "Between 1898 and 1903 Louisiana, North Carolina, Alabama, and Virginia imitated them, followed by Oklahoma and Georgia in 1907 and 1908."[1] The right to vote became tied to ownership of property and education.

"Of all the Southern states, North Carolina was the least discriminatory in its racial practices. For example, it sent a Negro to Congress during most of the 1880's and 1890's."[2]

Political, educational, economic, and transportation-related inequalities were common. The Black man in the South watched as the Republican party that had stood by him during the Civil War shifted to compromise and then to acceptance of the southern race system.

> The Compromise of 1877 revealed that the Republicans were unwilling to enforce the Reconstruction legislation in the South. During the 1880s, President Chester A. Arthur courted anti-black "independent" political organizations in the South in an effort to increase Republican strength. Not only did the party [that claimed to represent the freedman] fail to stop mob violence and disfranchisement, but it was a Republican Supreme Court that found the Civil Rights Act unconstitutional; and it was a Republican Congress that in 1890 repudiated campaign pledges by failing to pass the Lodge Federal Elections Bill.[3]

My father-in-law, who at the writing of this book is seventy-seven years old, grew up in the Deep South in the early 1900s. He easily recalls the horrors he experienced in the rural South, where the majority of Blacks lived in the United States during this time. The prospect of violence continually confronted him and he had to be constantly on guard.

The dangers associated with being Black were not restricted to the South. Leon Litwack writes:

> Legal and extralegal discrimination restricted northern Negroes in virtually every phase of existence. Where laws were lacking or ineffectual, public opinion provided its own remedies. Indeed, few held out any hope for the successful or peaceful integration of the Negro into a white-dominated society. . . .
>
> Most northerners, to the extent that they thought about it at all, rebelled at the idea of racial amalgamation or integration. Instead, they favored voluntary colonization, forced expulsion, or legal and social proscription.[4]

It's interesting that many Blacks of the late twentieth century would say that not much has changed. Public opinion still "provides its own remedies" to the problems of integration and equal rights and opportunities. Jawanza Kunjufu writes of the state of racial relations today in *Countering the Conspiracy to Destroy Black Boys*:

> To use the word conspiracy, which is an act of plotting together to harm someone, to describe certain aspects of our society is a strong indictment of the social fabric of this country. The conspiracy to destroy Black boys is very complex and interwoven. There are many contributors to the conspiracy, ranging from the very visible who are more obvious, to the less visible and silent partners who are more difficult to recognize.
>
> Those people who adhere to the doctrine of white racism, imperialism, and the white male supremacy are eas-

41

ier to recognize. Those people who actively promoted drugs and gang violence are active conspirators and easier to identify. What makes the conspiracy more complex are those people who do not plot together to destroy Black boys, but, through their indifference, perpetrate it. This passive group of conspirators consists of parents, educators, and white liberals who deny being racists, but through their silence allow institutional racism to continue.[5]

And Andrew Hacker writes:

Throughout this nation's history, race has always had a central role. Until recently, however, most notions concerning the races and relations between them either went unquestioned or remained relatively muted. As recently as a generation ago, white Americans in both the South and the North would say that so far as they could see their region had no overpowering racial problems. Most of them really wanted to believe that blacks and whites coexisted quite amiably; separately, to be sure, but that was a matter of mutual choice.

For almost a century after the abolition of slavery, America's black population subsisted under a system of controls. In the South, physical force was blatant and unabashed. The whims of a sheriff, an employer, even the driver of a bus, could hold black lives in thrall. In the North, intimidation and oppression were less explicit but nonetheless real. Fear of the police obviously helped to maintain this submission, for in those days precinct houses were less attentive to legal processes than they seem to be today. An equally effective control lay in the understanding that members of subordinate races did not touch or threaten their betters. This is not to suggest that black Americans were happy with their condition. Many were resentful, if not totally enraged. But given the panoply of power they faced, the most common posture was one of resignation: a minority with barely an avenue of appeal.[6]

With the implementation of Jim Crowism, racism became a way of life in the South and was having influence on the

North and West as well. There was a concerted effort in the South to maintain White supremacy and White solidarity and to do this, there was persistent propaganda about Blacks. They were, it was said, immoral, violent, and lazy. Politicians convinced their electorate that Blacks were advancing too quickly for the good of society and they won votes by coming up with ways to keep Blacks under control. This talk of needing to control Blacks invited and sanctioned extreme methods, such as lynchings, which were carried out for such "crimes" as testifying against Whites in court or attempting to vote. Between 1890 and 1900 there were 1,217 lynchings.

Whites easily accepted the propaganda. It seemed to fit with a sense of superiority that had developed in this country over the years since its founding. This ideology had already been seen in American overseas imperialism and perhaps was the natural reaction of the White American to the free African American.

Former White abolitionists seemed unable or unwilling to see and hear what was going on. They were weary, it seems, of the "Negro problem" and now it was no longer just a southern problem. Now that slavery had been abolished, the problem of justice for African Americans was a problem for the country to face. But instead of facing the problem and fighting the injustices, northern liberals were apathetic, and there was a quiet acceptance of segregation. There were even northern "scholars" who supported the southern racist doctrines, affirming that Blacks were a separate species, akin to apes.

This era for Blacks was a time of humiliation and exploitation as well as injustice and suffering. Quickly the Black person was separated from his White counterpart in every way. He had to ride in a separate railway car, drink from a separate water fountain, and enter public establishments through separate entrances. His labor was exploited through long hours and unfair wages.

Hacker says,

> Little attention was paid to the conditions under which black Americans lived. It was assumed, for example, that a docile pool would always be available for the arduous labors required by white society. No one thought to ask what domestic servants did after their working hours. Black Americans remained unobtrusive, and apparently uncomplaining, for all intents invisible to white eyes.
>
> These were placid years for white Americans. No serious movements or organized protests arose to upset white sensibilities. No talk of black power was in the air, and only the barest whispers of egalitarian aspirations could be heard. Black Americans knew they were regarded as marginal members of the nation, and realized that white America saw them as an alien appendage.[7]

As seemingly every effort of White America was aimed at rendering African Americans powerless and cowering, Blacks as a group became cautious and began to think in terms of quiet accommodation rather than open protest. This meant suppressing outward displays of cultural and racial distinctives so as not to disturb the majority. It also meant turning inward, finding the resources within the group for their own preservation and advancement. Rather than integration into the larger society, racial solidarity was stressed.

It was at this time that Booker T. Washington began advocating his accommodationist philosophy. A former slave, Washington became one of the most powerful men of the nineteenth and early twentieth centuries, whether Black or White. Authors Lincoln and Mamiya call him "the national Negro leader of his day." He worked to convince millions of African Americans that they could gain economic viability through self-help and the acceptance of middle-class values. Washington believed Blacks needed to stay in the South and focus on acquiring an agrarian-based education to equip them to become the best farmworkers. His conservative approach to racial equality and assimilation attracted many of the largest financiers, such as Andrew Carnegie, to invest in the Black community. Washington held strong ties to the Black church and was able to help strengthen their economic role in improving the lives of Blacks. His views on economics represented a microcosm of the leaders of the Black church of the early twentieth century.[8]

> Washington advocated a conciliatory and gradualist philosophy. He minimized the extent of race prejudice or discrimination and referred to southern whites as the black man's best friends. He held that discrimination and prejudice were basically the Negroes' own fault. . . . He believed that economic accumulation and the cultivation of morality were the methods best calculated to raise the black people's status in American society.[9]

The Great Migration

"After the Civil War and Emancipation, the major watershed in American black history was the Great Migration to Northern cities" that began in 1910 and reached full force in the 1930s.[10] "Migration of Southern black people searching for better conditions was not new. In the years since the Civil War there had been a steady drift of blacks to Southern urban centers, along with a trickle to the North."[11] "Between 1890 and 1910 the proportion of Negroes classified as urban by the United States census rose from about 20 to 27 percent. In the latter year there were a dozen cities that had over forty thousand Negroes.[12] Du Bois noted this growing northern movement as early as 1903.

Lerone Bennett writes:

> Why did this happen? Why did people move?
> They moved because the sheriff was mean, because planters were mean, because life was mean. They were

45

pushed by drought, boll weevils and tyranny, and they were pulled by the lure of employment in burgeoning wartime industries. Labor agents of Northern industrialists stimulated the movement; so did Robert Abbott and other editors who printed great big headlines of welcome: "GOOD-BYE DIXIE." New vistas, new hopes, new opportunities: these stimulated the most significant movement in the history of black Americans. Seen thus, as an explosion of hopes and fears, the Great Migration was a revolt, and that revolt continued through the sixties as a permanent element in the black protest.[13]

So Blacks left the tyranny and oppression of the South to follow the dream of equality and success in the North. In large part their dreams went unfulfilled. Blacks who moved into the North did not find the openness and freedom they had hoped for. In fact those who moved into the cities prior to World War I found themselves in a social setting where racial lines were tightly drawn. Though early on, Blacks who moved North were able to move into White neighborhoods, it wasn't long before this was prohibited in most cities, and Blacks were relegated to certain restricted neighborhoods. But their economic condition improved as they became laborers in northern industries. Bennett writes, "In the big cities of the North blacks emancipated themselves, casting off the garments of slavery and the feudal South."[14] So they continued to come. Nearly half a million Blacks left the South soon after World War I. The Black population of northern cities such as New York, Chicago, and Detroit more than tripled during the first twenty years of the Great Migration.

My grandfather, born in 1900, was one of those who left the South during that time to work in northern industry. Because of economic pressures, he came to the North to do better for himself and his family. He was a man of dignity who raised seven children in the heart of the inner city.

The New Negro

Within this context the fledging cultural nationalist movement began, led by W. E. B. Du Bois, James Weldon Johnson, and the now infamous Marcus Garvey.

W. E. B. Du Bois

W. E. B. Du Bois (1868–1963) was one of the most profound and influential African American thinkers of the late nineteenth and early twentieth centuries, becoming the first African American to earn a Ph.D. from Harvard University. A prolific writer and speaker, he envisioned that an elite corps of Black intellectuals, whom he called the "Talented Tenth," would lead the masses of Black people to greater prosperity and acceptance within the majority community. His activism was in sharp contrast with the accommodationist philosophy of Booker T. Washington, and the two remained rivals throughout their lives.

In 1905, Du Bois organized the Niagara Movement, a group of African American leaders who shared his perspective in terms of the achievement of total economic and political rights for Blacks and who disagreed with Washington's accommodationist strategy. For about five years the Niagara Movement served as a voice for a segment of the Black community, denouncing racism and all its ramifications in America.

Washington, however, had greater success in attracting supporters from the Black and White communities. His accommodationist approach was easier for Whites to accept and, as a result, he received their financial backing.

In 1910 Du Bois helped organize the NAACP and became its director of publications and research. For nearly twenty-five years he edited the *Crisis*, the NAACP's official publication.

A major focus for Du Bois was Pan-Africanism, an ideology that espoused an emotional commitment to the Black race and to Africa as the fatherland. Du Bois organized a series of Pan-African conferences and, along with Marcus Garvey, set forth an aggressive Pan-Africanist agenda that he hoped would culminate in a unified empire of people of African descent. However, due to many personal and philosophical differences, Du Bois and Garvey would become political enemies.

Du Bois would eventually become so disillusioned with the American democratic system that in the 1960s, he joined the Communist party and became a citizen of Ghana, where he died in 1963 on the eve of the Civil Rights March on Washington.[15]

Marcus Garvey

Marcus Garvey was a charismatic leader who believed the Black man's ultimate salvation was in leaving this "god-forsaken land" to the White man and returning to his roots in Africa. Through colorful processions that attracted a following, Garvey glorified Mother Africa and spread his philosophy of racial pride and cultural solidarity. In 1914 he founded the Universal Negro Improvement Association. He taught that blackness meant strength, beauty, and manliness; that African Americans had a noble heritage; and that they should take pride in their accomplishments.

Garvey argued that it was futile to protest against racism or try to integrate the United States. He believed the only solution was to emigrate to Africa. Although he was not successful in attracting mass support for this exodus, his Pan-African rallies galvanized the Black community. Garvey's followers asserted that no matter where they lived, they would always have an attachment to Africa and would work toward self-government for oppressed Blacks around the world.

Garvey denounced the integrationist strategies of the NAACP and said the lighter-skinned upper-class Blacks, such as Du Bois, had betrayed their identities. Garvey's leadership flourished for several years and brought a renewed hope to millions of Black Americans.[16]

Strong opposition from such men as Du Bois, inept business dealings, and his conviction in 1923 of mail fraud and his deportation in 1927 as an undesirable alien brought about Garvey's decline. By then, however, he had succeeded in raising the level of consciousness of the Black masses, creating a national Black organization, and helping make White Americans more aware of the Black culture.

Racial Solidarity

Before Garvey founded his Universal Negro Improvement Association, Du Bois had established the NAACP in 1910 and Booker T. Washington had been instrumental in founding the National Urban League in 1911. Despite the antagonism between the two founders, these two organizations together served the Black population in two important areas. The NAACP provided legal defense for Blacks who were victims of race riots or unjust judicial proceedings. They also were successful in securing public support for their crusade against lynchings, which gradually declined in number. The Urban League was mainly involved in securing fair treatment in the area of employment.

A new sense of racial pride and solidarity was sweeping through the Black community. There was progress to be proud of and leaders to emulate. While the NAACP and Urban League were leading the way on the political and economic fronts, there was movement and then a literal explosion in the arts as well. Suddenly Black writers, painters, and musicians were freely expressing their cultural pride in their art.

In 1925 Alain Locke, editor of the special Harlem issue of *Survey Graphic*, coined the term "New Negro." The New

Negro, according to Locke, who was the first Black Rhodes scholar and professor of philosophy at Howard University, was not like the old Negro: docile, passive, and ready to do whatever the master wanted. This New Negro had developed a sense of adequacy, a knowledge that Blacks were culturally as advanced, if not more so, than their White counterparts.

> The New Negro was militant and proud of his race, desired to perpetrate the group identity and yet participate fully in American society. The New Negro protested and demanded his rights of citizenship and insisted upon the value of a black subculture. Intellectually and artistically, he believed that Negroes should have pride in their past and their traditions; and by using the themes from Negro life and history as an inspiration for his literary work, the New Negro intended to enrich the culture of America.
>
> The ethnic dualism and cultural pluralism of the New Negro movement or Harlem Renaissance had diverse origins. Interest in the race's past had been growing since the beginning of the century. The first courses in black history were introduced in a few black colleges about the time of the First World War.[17]

James Weldon Johnson

James Weldon Johnson, considered the father of the Harlem Renaissance, was an artistic, literary, and political genius. With Du Bois, Johnson led the NAACP during its early years and was its executive director from 1920 to 1930. His influence through the arts shaped the Black person's cultural consciousness during the first half of the twentieth century.[18]

This was an interesting period when it was fashionable for the White elite to hobnob with Black intellectuals. Whites were attracted to Harlem where they could spend an evening enjoying jazz or being entertained by Blacks at the Cotton Club, which was for Whites only.

Writers W. E. B. Du Bois, James Weldon Johnson, and Langston Hughes became household names, not just in the Black community but across America. The Black man was now beginning (for the first time since the days of Reconstruction) to feel good about himself.

This era of renewed enthusiasm was short-lived, however. Blacks in other parts of the country, specifically the South, were still in the throes of Jim Crowism. And the arrival of the Great Depression meant that White Americans could no longer "indulge" the Negro. They suddenly became completely self-centered. The fun was over and the Harlem Renaissance only a memory.

Urban Adjustment and the Church

The patterns of adjustment to life in the North of the rural southern Negro are fascinating. Although Blacks were migrating within the confines of one country, when they arrived in a northern city, the cultural adaptation they needed to make for survival was great. Two institutions that were crucial to a successful transformation were the church and the matriarchal family. Both entities functioned to help Blacks adjust to the dismal realities of urban life.

Quoting August Meier:

The high incidence of matrifocal families, whether or not the pattern had African roots, was a legacy of the plantations. Its persistence was encouraged, however, by complications of urban life. When the migrants moved into the cities, they found that women could obtain and hold jobs more easily than men; women became domestic servants and their work was steadier and commonly more remunerative than that of men. In a society where the man is regarded as responsible for the support of his family, black

51

men often felt inadequate. The results were frequent separations and many households where the mother or grandmother was the central figure. While it is customary to look upon the high incidence of such households as a sign of social disorganization among lower-class Negroes, there is another way to view the matter. The matrifocal family pattern can be regarded as a stabilizing influence in the lives of its members, as a creative response to the circumstances under which black people found themselves, first on the plantation and then in the urban ghetto. Economic factors are not wholly responsible for the matrifocal family, for once established, such forms of institutional life tend to perpetuate themselves.[19]

The rural Black church became an urban storefront. Often these were sects that featured a religious frenzy of Sunday worship, which allowed the participants to escape briefly their otherwise difficult lives. These churches, led by ambitious but not necessarily well-trained men and women, provided an emotional release for their parishioners and became the key bridging agents for Blacks arriving from the South.

The Baptist church, especially within the urban context, tended to be the dominant forum of religious expression. Such prominent churches as Abyssinian Baptist in New York and Pilgrim Baptist in Chicago formed bridges between the land that migrating Blacks had grown up in and a land that was totally foreign to them. Between 1916 and 1926 membership in northern Baptist churches increased by 200 percent.[20] A.M.E. churches also had a 124 percent increase in the number of churches and 83 percent increase in membership in the northern cities of Chicago, Detroit, Cincinnati, Philadelphia, and Baltimore.[21]

The church became the one constant in the transition from the rural South to the urban North. The church observed and preserved the customs and traditions of the homeland. It also provided a network that enabled the community to access educational, economic, and political opportunities. The Black church was the primary forum for the dissemination of information to the community and it shaped public opinion. Even today the Black church holds this status.

The Rise of Black Denominations

— 4 —

One day in class a student asked me, "Prof, how did we get all these denominations?" Here's the short answer:

- *Common heritage.* Many groups came to America during the religious persecution of the mid-1800s and built networks of churches founded on a common identity and background.
- *Theological distinctives.* One example is the Conservative Baptist denomination, which was formed in the 1920s and 1930s in response to the liberalism they perceived was becoming more rampant in the denomination with which they were affiliated.
- *Missiological initiatives.* One example is the Baptist General Conference, which has a heavy missiological emphasis, having formed its own world mission board out of a commitment to see itself reproduced. The churches of this denomination also share a common heritage.

One cannot understand the Black church without looking at the influence of the historic Black denominations. There are seven major historic Black denominations, which claim a membership of nearly twenty million. This represents about two-thirds of all the Blacks in the United States.[1]

Any serious student of African American history knows the Black church has no rival in terms of the institutional loyalty of its members. As the only stable and coherent institution to emerge from slavery, Black churches were not only dominant in their communities, but they became the womb of Black culture and major social institutions.

While the social processes of migration, urbanization, and differentiation have diminished some aspects of their centrality and dominance, Black churches have continued influencing the spheres of politics, economics, education, and culture. This involvement has helped the churches remain a relevant, vibrant voice in our society.

The Black denominations have served as a resource to the local church and its minister. The seven major Black denominations can be broken down into three major theological camps—Baptist, Methodist, and Pentecostal. Let's look at the Baptists first.

The Baptists

Today there are eight significant Black Baptist denominations in the United States: National Baptist Convention, U.S.A., Inc., National Baptist Convention of America, Progressive National Baptist Convention, Lott Carey Baptist Foreign Mission Convention, National Primitive Baptist Convention, U.S.A., United Free Will Baptist Church, National Baptist Evangelical Life and Soul Saving Assembly of the U.S.A., and Free for All Missionary Baptist Church, Inc. There are also large numbers of Black Baptists who are part of the Southern Baptist Convention and the American Baptist Churches in the U.S.A. Many Black Baptist churches that affiliate with one of these denominations have dual membership in one of the national Black Baptist denominations.

When Black Baptist churches were first being organized in the last half of the eighteenth century, they were usually located on White plantations in the South. In the North, abolitionist missionary societies were being formed by free Blacks. It was common for the Black churches of this era to be associated with a White Baptist church, and it was not long before the Black leaders began to chafe under the unequal and restrictive treatment they received from the White denominations. Early in the Reconstruction period, there was a drive to organize a separate national Black Baptist convention.

Black Baptist Conventions

The earliest Black Baptist associations were regional organizations that came together for mutual support and evangelism. Providence Association was established in Ohio in 1836, Union Association in Ohio in 1836, Wood River Association in Illinois in 1839, and Amherstburg Association in Canada and in Michigan in 1841. In 1840 the American Baptist Missionary Convention was organized at Abyssinian Baptist Church in New York for the purpose of education, evangelism, and racial solidarity. Most of the Black conventions of this time worked for the abolition of slavery and were part of the Underground Railroad. The American Baptist Missionary convention was a regional group that served New England and the Middle Atlantic States.

A similarly large association was formed in Illinois in 1839. The Wood River Association was instrumental in bringing together other regional associations from eight states into one body, known as the Consolidated American Baptist Missionary Convention (CABMC). In 1868 it reported a membership of 100,000. "The first national effort at consolidation . . . foundered on the shoals of inadequate financial support and internal class conflicts between the educated northern blacks and the southern ex-slaves on such issues as emotional fervor and political activism."[2]

When this first national convention dissolved, three other organizations quickly came into existence:

- Baptist Foreign Mission Convention of the United States
- American National Baptist Convention
- National Baptist Educational Convention of the U.S.A.

In 1880 Rev. W. W. Colley organized the *Baptist Foreign Mission Convention of the United States of America*. Rev. Colley had been a missionary to West Africa under the Southern Baptist Convention. When the interests of the White convention dwindled and they closed their mission work in Africa, Colley returned home to arouse the passion of his Black brothers and sisters for missionary work on that continent.

He was successful in organizing churches from ten southern states who formed the convention in 1880 in Montgomery, Alabama. They immediately sent six missionaries to Liberia and over the next few years developed a significant missions program, supporting missionaries in Africa and other parts of the world. They also published a magazine, *The African Missions*.

The Baptist Foreign Mission Convention was active in the United States as well, with a particular concern for the problems associated with the use of tobacco and alcohol.

The *American National Baptist Convention* was formed in 1886 by Rev. William J. Simmons. Rev. Simmons was driven by two commitments—to unify Black Baptists in an effort to evangelize Africa and to cooperate with White Baptists in doing so. He was reacting to the strong resistance of the Baptist Foreign Mission Convention to joining White Christians in missions work. Ironically, northern White Baptists opposed the formation of this convention—of any Black convention—believing that Blacks still needed the guidance that a White convention would offer.

Churches from more than twenty states were represented at the first meeting of the American National Baptist Convention. This convention claimed a membership of more than one million. It was committed to Christian missions, especially in Africa, and in the furthering of Black education in the United States.

The third national organization to be formed after CABMC went out of existence was the *National Baptist Educational Convention*. In 1893 Rev. W. Bishop Johnson of Washington, D.C., called together delegates from all over the country to form an organization that would concern itself with the education and training of clergy and missionaries. Up until this time Black Baptists had depended entirely on White institutions for their training and materials. Rev. Johnson, who had long been involved in education, believed it was time for the Black churches to oversee their own training. The convention helped to fund the education of young men and women and to locate positions for graduates. This commitment would eventually form the impetus behind the founding of several colleges and seminaries.

In 1895, through the efforts of several leaders who believed a unified national convention would benefit the Black Baptist church, the three organizations came together to form the *National Baptist Convention, U.S.A.* (NBC). Rev. E. C. Morris of Arkansas was chosen the first president. Boards were formed that reflected the interests of the three cooperating conventions: boards of foreign missions, home missions, and education. Later other boards would be established: Baptist Training Union board, a publishing board, and a benefit association board.

The convention was particularly proud of its publishing board. Until soon after the creation of the National Baptist Convention, Black Baptists had depended on the White American Baptist Publication Society for its teaching materials. But after the Society invited Black writers to contribute to its publications and then, because of pressure from the Southern Baptists, rescinded that offer, the National Baptist Convention determined that it should be responsible for and produce its own materials. Thus the publishing board was established with the purpose of providing training materials written by Blacks to be used by teachers in Black churches. It served other purposes as well. It provided employment and was a money-making business venture. "There was great rejoicing when the Publishing Board put out its first issue of *The Sunday School Teacher* and quarterlies in January 1897."[3]

At its founding, the National Baptist Convention, U.S.A., claimed one million members from eight thousand churches. By 1906 there were more than seventeen thousand ministers associated with this convention and in 1915 they reported three million members.

It was not long, however, before there was discontent particularly among those original members who were concerned that foreign missions have top priority in the work of the convention and that they cooperate with White Baptists, especially in the area of missions and the use of published materials. The majority group disagreed, believing that a completely separate Black convention was essential for racial progress.

The issue that finally brought matters to a head was the moving of the foreign mission board headquarters from

Richmond, Virginia, to Louisville, Kentucky. The result was that in 1897 a good number of members withdrew from the National Baptist Convention and formed their own convention—*Lott Carey Foreign Missionary Convention.* Carey had been the first Black missionary to Africa. He established a church in Liberia in 1822, dying there in 1828.

The primary commitment of the organizers of the Lott Carey Foreign Missionary Convention was foreign missions. Their differences with the National Baptist Convention seemed to align with their differences in class and ideology, those who withdrew being the better educated. As had happened before in the history of the Black church, differences in class and education had caused disunity.

In 1905 the two conventions reconciled but they continue to exist independently of each other. They now cooperate in their foreign missions program.

Yet another split occurred in 1915, when the National Baptist Convention, Unincorporated, was formed. This group was later called the *National Baptist Convention of America* (NBCA). A disagreement developed and simmered for several years between two factions of the National Baptist Convention. The dispute centered on the control of the publishing board.

R. H. Boyd was the secretary of the publishing board and under his leadership it had become a successful and prosperous business. Its prosperity, however, was not shared with the other boards of the convention.

Boyd built a new facility for the publishing entity on his own property in Nashville, Tennessee, and he had the publishing board incorporated in that state. This would have strong ramifications later when the National Baptist Convention tried to prevent Boyd from claiming ownership of the publishing board. The convention had not been incorporated and had no legal claim to the publishing board.

The courts determined that the publishing board, a legal entity, could affiliate with any organization of its choosing.

In 1915 in Chicago the Boyd faction broke away from the rest of the National Baptist Convention, of which Morris was still president. The new group, eventually called the National Baptist Convention of America, took the publishing board with it and decided to affiliate with the Lott Carey Foreign Missionary Convention for its missions work. Later they organized their own missions board.

The focus of the NBCA was on prohibition, evangelism, education, civil rights, urban social services, and the antilynching campaign. It continues to be the second largest Black Baptist convention. In 1997 its membership numbered 3.5 million.[4]

In 1961 another group broke off from the National Baptist Convention U.S.A. Those who formed the *Progressive National Baptist Convention* (PNBC) had two disputes with the leadership of the NBCUSA. They opposed the continued tenure of the president, Rev. J. H. Jackson, and they disagreed with the conservative stance he took on the civil rights movement. Rev. Jackson had called for moderation in civil rights, believing the strategy of Martin Luther King Jr. too aggressive and therefore damaging to the progress of the Black race.

The opposing group was originally led by Rev. Dr. Gardner C. Taylor and included Martin Luther King Sr., Martin Luther King Jr., Ralph Abernathy, and Benjamin Mays. When, in 1961, they actually formed their own convention, Rev. L. V. Booth was elected president.

The dispute over Jackson's reelection in 1960 actually was settled in court. A new election was held and Jackson was reelected. The dissenting officers, it is said, though they called for unity after the election, were removed from office.

The following year thirty-three people gathered in Cincinnati for the first meeting of the Progressive National Baptist Convention. The programs of this convention focus on education, job training, and the family. They were active in the civil rights movement of the 1960s. The convention has a full-time general secretary who oversees the work of the convention. They have no publishing house. Many of the PNBC churches are also affiliated with White conventions. In 1997 they reportedly had 2.5 million members.

Despite the fact that groups have broken off from it, the National Baptist Convention, U.S.A., remains the largest Black Baptist convention. It is the largest organization of Black Americans in existence, claiming a membership of 8.2 million. It holds a loose affiliation with its member churches, allowing each of them to operate according to Baptist polity and autonomy.

Other Conventions

Black members broke away from the White Primitive Baptists after Emancipation, forming their own association in 1870. It was not until 1906, however, that the convention became national and was called the *National Primitive Baptist Convention, U.S.A.* They have an estimated membership of 250,000.

The *United Free Will Baptist Church* was organized in 1870 and has approximately 100,000 members. The *National Baptist Evangelical Life and Soul Saving Assembly of the U.S.A.* was organized in 1920 and currently has 50,000 members, and the *Free for All Missionary Baptist Church, Inc.*, formed in 1955, has 10,000 members.

The Methodists

There are three predominant Black Methodist movements in the United States: African Methodist Episcopal Church, African Methodist Episcopal Zion Church, and the Christian Methodist Episcopal Church.

As we saw in chapter 1, Richard Allen is considered the founder of the Black denominations in America. The movement of Free African Societies that was begun by Allen and Absalom Jones spread to other cities. They were religious societies, formed for the protection and advancement of Black interests and the abolition of slavery. In 1816 these societies came together to form the *African Methodist Episcopal Church* (AME), with Allen appointed as the first bishop. Thus the AME convention was the first organization of Black churches in the United States.

> The doctrine and polity of the church, set forth in *The Book of Discipline*, were modeled after the original Methodist Episcopal Church, as was the case with each of the major black Methodist bodies. Their original dispute [with the Methodist Episcopal Church] was not with matters of belief or structure, but with the failure of the white church to honor its own commitments to love and brotherhood and respect for all of God's children.[5]

Sadly, race superseded theology in separating the Black and White Methodist movements in this country.

Historically (particularly in most of the twentieth century), Methodists have been perceived by African Americans as the denomination that attracted more middle- to upper-class Black parishioners, while the Pentecostal or Church of God in Christ movement tended to attract, with its high emphasis on emotionalism, African Americans from lower socioeconomic positions. Baptist churches seemed to attract many working- and middle-class individuals. Methodist churches, however, especially earlier in their organizational life, tried to reach any who would listen to the basic message of Methodism and of the spiritual graces or discipline needed to become all God wants a person to be.

The motto of the AME Church is "God our Father, Christ our Redeemer, man our brother." This group has from the beginning assumed two important functions: providing education and ministering to people in this country and the world through missions.

When the denomination was first founded, ministers were encouraged to receive training for their positions. The AME Church was instrumental in the founding of several colleges and other institutions of learning. In 1856 the Methodist Episcopal Church established Wilberforce College in Ohio as a Black college. This college was transferred to the AME Church in 1863.

Before the end of the Civil War, the AME Church had begun mission work in the South, winning many slaves to Christ. It also has had an effective missionary outreach in Africa and the Caribbean.

By 1896 the AME Church had grown to 450,000 members. It is still the largest Black Methodist church with 3.5 million members in 1997.

The *African Methodist Episcopal Zion Church* (AMEZ) developed separately from the AME Church. When the AMEZ organized in 1820, they chose not to join "the Allenites," as they were called. In 1848 they added "Zion" to their name to distinguish themselves from the Philadelphia group.

The first AME Zion church was organized in 1796 by a group of Blacks in New York who were worshiping with a White congregation, the John Street Methodist Episcopal Church. The Black members felt the need to have their own church and began meeting separately. They established Zion Church and built their own building. They were independent, except for pastoral supervision given by the White conference.

In 1820 they broke away from the White Methodist Episcopal Church conference because of the paternalism and racism they felt. They formed the African Methodist Episcopal Church. In 1822 James Varick was chosen the first bishop. By 1896 they had 350,000 members and in 1997 1.2 million members were reported.

Early on, the church had a commitment to missions, sending missionaries to the South as well as to South America, Africa, and the West Indies.

The AMEZ Church became known as "The Freedom Church" because of their work for the abolition of slavery and because of members such as Harriet Tubman, Sojourner Truth, and Frederick Douglass—a licensed AMEZ preacher. Many members were involved in the Underground Railroad.[6]

The *Christian Methodist Episcopal Church* (CME) was founded in the South in the post-slavery period, later than the other two major Methodist groups. The CME originally was called the Colored Methodist Episcopal Church. The name was changed in 1954.

The people who organized the CME Church had been members of the Methodist Episcopal Church, South.

> Their departure from the M.E. Church, South, was not only a protest of the segregated and demeaning treatment to which northern and southern blacks alike were subjected, but an explicit declaration of self-determination by a new citizenry, almost all of whom were without experience beyond the conditions of slavery.[7]

The White church had encouraged the Blacks to organize their own conference, helping them from 1866 to 1870 to prepare for it and making provision for ordaining their ministers. The separation was friendly, and at the first meeting of the new conference, one of the resolutions was to stay on good terms with the M.E. Church, a relationship that still continues today.

The first general conference was held in Tennessee in 1870. Two men, former slaves, were chosen as bishops—William H. Miles and Richard H. Vanderhorst. The White conference transferred certain church properties to the

Black group with the condition that they would not be involved in any political activity, a condition to which they agreed. The mandate of the church, however, calls for "the salvation of sinners and the liberation of the oppressed from all forms of human bondage."

The CME Church grew slowly, with 103,000 members in 1890 and 900,000 in 1989. The church was initially limited to the South but now there are CME churches throughout the United States and abroad.

Black United Methodists, though not a separate denomination, are a significant and influential bloc of Methodists within the United States. Currently they comprise 330,000 members of a denomination of 8.5 million members. Today out of the 51 bishops in the United Methodist Church, ten are Black. They also named the first female bishop among Methodist groups—Leontine T. C. Kelly, a Black woman.

Black Pentecostals

The modern Pentecostal movement in the United States began for both Black and White people at the Azusa Street Revival held in Los Angeles (1906–1909). This revival was led by William Seymour, a Black Holiness preacher. Thus, Pentecostalism began as an interracial movement, from which Whites subsequently withdrew to form their own churches.

The predominant Black Pentecostal denomination is *Church of God in Christ* (COGIC), with an estimated membership of 5.5 million. It was formed at the turn of the century out of the Holiness tradition by Charles Mason. Born in 1866 to former slaves, Mason was raised Baptist and became a Baptist minister after studying at Arkansas Bible College. He was dismissed from his church because of his belief in the doctrine of sanctification but continued to preach as an evangelist. In 1897 he joined with Elder

Charles Jones to begin a work in Lexington, Kentucky. In 1906 the congregation erected its first building and named it St. Paul Church of God in Christ, the first church of this denomination.

"While in attendance at the Azusa Street Revival in 1907 for five weeks, Elders Mason, D. J. Young, and W. J. Jegter were baptized 'with the Holy Ghost and fire'" and spoke in tongues.[8] Mason was overwhelmed by this experience, which confirmed for him the validity of his teaching concerning sanctification. Elder Jones, however, did not agree that a second baptism of the Holy Spirit is needed. As a result of the disagreement, Jones assumed leadership of the non-Pentecostal segment of the movement, which became the *Church of Christ Holiness, U.S.A.* The larger group remained with Mason, who taught that speaking in tongues is evidence of the indwelling of the Holy Spirit.

In November 1907 Elder Mason convened the first Pentecostal General Assembly of COGIC in Memphis. Representatives of twelve churches were in attendance. At this meeting Mason was designated "General Overseer and Chief Apostle" with absolute authority in all matters of doctrine and church organization.

For a few years the denomination consisted of an interracial mix of Black and White Pentecostals. This lasted until 1914, when several White ministers, ordained by Mason, formed the Assemblies of God.

The expansion of the COGIC was phenomenal and mainly the result of Mason's ability to develop leaders. It has become a mainly urban church. Between the mid-1920s and the early 1960s, membership rose from 50,000 to 400,000. Since then it has escalated to a membership now of 5.5 million members, making it the second largest Black denomination.

Following Mason's death in 1961 the church entered a period of turmoil. A power struggle arose between Senior

Bishop Ozro T. Jones Sr. and the executive board. This struggle lasted for four years. In 1968 a court-ordered constitutional convention was called. At this convention a formal constitution was drafted, defining denominational offices and the authority each would possess. Later that year Bishop James Patterson Sr., Mason's son-in-law, was elected presiding bishop, a position he held until his death in 1989.

COGIC is emphasizing foreign missions more and more. Since the end of the civil rights era, the focus has been primarily in Africa and the Caribbean. Of the Black denominations that are heavily urban, this group reaches the broadest spectrum of people and has had overwhelming success in giving hope to the poor and downcast.

The Black Preacher

Undisputed Leader

Henry Mitchell, former professor of theology at Rochester Divinity School, said, "The central figure in the black church is the black preacher. He has no exact counterpart in the white church, and to attempt to see the white minister on the same plane is to risk confusion, for the black preacher includes a dimension peculiar to the black experience."[1]

Tony Evans writes, "It should be little wonder that the Black preacher has perpetually served as a father figure to Black people, seeing to their welfare in all spheres of life whether they were social, political, economic, or the traditionally recognized spiritual aspects of life. Such a position is not unknown to biblical revelation. The New Testament church leaders had little trouble viewing their followers from a parent-child perspective."[2]

As a product of the ghetto of the 1950s and 1960s, I saw in operation the validity of these statements. The preacher commanded the respect and obedience of his congregation. He (in those days in my Baptist heritage I rarely saw

71

female ministers) was the most powerful man in our community. Even today the Black preacher retains most of that prominence.

What makes the Black preacher unique? What we discussed in chapter 1 about the Black church's African roots provides a substantial portion of the answer.

Descendants of Tribal Priests

As the Black church's historical origin stemmed from its African heritage, the counterpart of the Black preacher can be found in African traditional religion. The African priest brought with him into slavery an oral tradition through which he preserved the history and culture of the tribe. Through his expertise in storytelling, he became a link for his fellow slaves between the past and the present and between the spiritual and the mundane. In his role as priest on the plantation, he comforted, encouraged, and helped the slave community relate to God.

H. Beecher Hicks, in *Images of the Black Preacher*, writes, "The Negro priest, therefore, early became an important figure on the plantation and found his function as the interpreter of the supernatural, the comforter of the sorrowing, and as the one who expressed, rudely but picturesquely, the longing and disappointment and resentment of a stolen people."[3]

It is unfortunate that many within the European American Community as well as the African American community do not acknowledge the influence of Africa on the religious foundation of Black Americans. Following this reasoning, the Christianity that evolved among Blacks is assumed to be of domestic origin. Yet a close examination of the Black church makes evident the fallacy of this assertion. Look, for example, at the direct correlation between the focus on the oral, informal teaching/learning model of the African priest, whose primary function was to recite the history of the clan, and the highly dialogical approach to preaching currently in use in the Black church. Because the Black preacher's roots are in his African past, the preeminence of the priest/preacher as the interpreter of culture parallels the priest's role in African tradition. This relationship with tradition is the foundation of the characteristics we recognize as peculiar to the Black preacher.

One role the priest brought from Africa was that of the tribe's benevolent father. This role of father figure was particularly evident in Black churches of the nineteenth and early twentieth centuries. The congregation looked to the preacher for help and wisdom in all aspects of life. He was the link to the wider Black community, and in many cases to the White community, and to the political arena. He interpreted community events for his members and helped them formulate opinions, take a stand for justice, and relate their faith to daily life. The preacher as father figure can still be seen in many African American churches today; however, this role is not as strong or as evident as it was twenty or thirty years ago.

The African priestly heritage endowed the Black preacher with the responsibility to represent his congregation before God. Since God is a comprehensive part of all of life, the Black preacher traditionally represented God's presence and leadership in every aspect of life. His role was critical as the spiritual, parental, and wise guide of his charges.

The presence of the priest provided the cohesiveness for the tribe, or church, in America. The preacher was the point person around whom relationships in the group revolved. He facilitated relationships between individuals and between the group and God. Albert J. Raboteau in his book *Slave Religion* writes:

Presiding over slave baptisms, funerals, and weddings was the slave preacher, leader of the slave's religious life and influential figure in the slave community. Usually illiterate, the slave preacher often had native wit and unusual eloquence. Licensed or unlicensed, with or without permission, preachers held prayer meetings, preached and ministered in a difficult situation. Carefully watched and viewed with suspicion, the preacher had to straddle the conflict between the demands of conscience and the orders of the masters.[4]

Anderson Edwards reflected on the difficulty he experienced as a slave preacher in Texas. "I have been preachin' the gospel and farmin' since slavery time. . . . When I starts preachin' I couldn't read or write and had to preach massa told me and he say tell them niggers iffen they obeys the massa they goes to heaven but I knowed there's something better for them, but daren't tell them 'cept on the sly. That I done lots I tell 'em iffen they keeps prayin' the Lord will set 'em free."[5]

Being a slave preacher was not only a place of privilege but a place of danger. As spokesmen for the community, slave preachers found their masters monitoring their words carefully. Any hint of rebellion or expression of the need for unity would lead to immediate repercussions.

Raboteau wrote:

The slave preacher who verged too close on a gospel of equality within ear shot of whites was in trouble. Sarah Ford told how "One day Uncle Lew preachin' and he say, De Lawd make everyone to come in unity and on de level, both white and black. When Massa Charles hears 'bout it, he don't like it none, and de next mornin' Old Uncle Jake git Uncle Lew and put him out in the field with de rest." Henry Clay Bruce retold the story of an old preacher named Uncle Tom Ewing, "Who was praying on one occasion, after the close of his sermon, in the church near Jacob Vennable's place. . . . The old fellow got warmed up, and used the words free indeed, free from work, free from white folks, free from everything. After the meeting closed, Jacob Vennable, who sat in front of the pulpit, took Tom to task and threatened to have his license revoked if he ever used such language in public."[6]

To be a Black preacher was to live with contradiction. A Black minister, although held in high esteem by his congregation, was still a "boy" in his master's eyes. Like most Blacks, he was only property and not worthy of any special treatment.

By the end of the Civil War, the Black preacher's role included that of educator, liberator, political leader, advocate, and spiritual leader. Unlike the White preacher, his status did not depend on formal education. Rather it hung on his ability to preach the Word, to represent his followers before God, and to be their representative before the White world that often humiliated their personhood and physically violated them.

The Call to Preach

Isaac Lane was a licensed slave preacher/exhorter for fellow slaves under the auspices of the Methodist Episcopal Church, South. After the war he participated in the conferences of Black Methodists that the White bishops organized in 1867 to keep more Blacks from exiting the church (two-thirds of the slave membership had left during the Civil War). Lane describes his experience as a slave preacher in *The Autobiography of Bishop Isaac Lane*:

> Shortly after my conversion, I was overcome with a feeling that I ought to preach. I strove for months to get rid of it, but without success. I went to a man in whose piety and Christian virtue I had much confidence and made known my struggle and the feeling that was then strong upon me. He gave me his sympathy and directed me to a certain preacher for counsel and aid; but this man did not believe in Negroes preaching, and gave me no encouragement.

75

I next sought the advice of a colored man whom the Methodists had helped. He was a pure Christian man, and he told me that if God had really called me to preach He surely knew His own business better than man and advised me now to trust God. . . . I sent in my petition to a Quarterly Conference of the Methodist Episcopal Church South, for license to preach. . . . The committee explained that the church did not believe it proper to grant license to Negroes to preach. . . . During the civil war the attitude of the Southern Methodist church toward granting license to Negroes to preach had undergone some changes and so I appeared again for a license to preach. This time I was granted my request.[7]

Although this type of discrimination was prevalent, it was not limited to this time period. The National Association of Evangelicals and the National Black Evangelical Association sponsored a Convocation on Racism in January 1995 to deal with the problem that still plagues the American evangelical church, that of racism and the need for racial reconciliation.

The call to be a preacher is different for a Black person than it has traditionally been for a White minister. A White person usually feels called to preach and goes through formal biblical and theological training. Ordination comes later, after the training is complete and the preaching ministry has begun.

When a Black person gets called by God to preach, the pattern is different. He has an inner sense of God's call, which he makes known to a group of recognized church leaders. He is examined and ordained by this group and enters the ministry. Formal training comes, if at all, after a preacher has begun his ministry. Today the pattern is changing slowly in the Black community. Yet the above pattern remains the predominant path to ministry there.[8]

Booker T. Washington said this about the call:

In the earlier days of freedom almost every colored man who learned to read would receive "a call to preach" within a few days after he began reading. At my home in West Virginia the process of being called to the ministry was a very interesting one. Usually the "call" came when the individual was sitting in church. Without warning the one called would fall upon the floor as if struck by a bullet, and would lie there for hours, speechless and motionless. Then the news would spread all through the neighborhood that this individual had received a "call." If he were inclined to resist the summons, he would fall or be made to fall a second or third time. In the end he always yielded to the call. While I wanted an education badly, I confess that in my youth I had a fear that when I had learned to read and write well I would receive one of these "calls"; but, for some reason, my call never came.[9]

Educated for Ministry

As slavery ended, the preacher already held the preeminent position in the community. The Black community, and Whites as well, considered the preacher to be the one who held up the moral and spiritual backbone of Black culture. Because the position was so respected, it attracted the most talented people to it, and these people usually proved worthy of the esteem they received. Many preachers, who before their call had had no formal theological education, sought to improve themselves through schooling.

Some of the first Black schools were seminaries, established by the churches to produce an educated clergy. Schools such as Payne Theological Seminary and Wilberforce University, both affiliated with the African Methodist Episcopal Church, began with the primary purpose of training ministers.

Among the People

Perhaps the peculiar genius of the Black preacher derives from the fact that he has never been far from the peo-

77

ple. He rose from among them as someone they knew and trusted, someone God had raised up. People referred to his credentials as "gifts," since they had been developed from childhood within the context of community. When he made good as a preacher, the community shared in his accomplishment. When they rewarded him for his faithfulness, it was a vicarious expression of the satisfaction the people felt with their own attainments.

The preacher was more than a leader and a pastor. He stood against adversity and oppression and symbolized success. Born out of the travail of slavery, the Black church became the bedrock for one's spiritual journey and the journey to freedom. Because of the oppressive policy and actions of a post-slavery government, apparently only concerned with the political, economic, and social agenda of the White majority, the Black church—and especially the Black preacher—forged a new agenda amidst the prevailing racism and prejudice. The preacher adopted the role of liberator, giving his people vision and hope. This role of liberator is uniquely identified with the Black preacher. He was responsible before God to do everything possible to see that God's people could grow.

As the Black church moved into the urban context, the preacher as liberator became the predominant model of the Black preacher's leadership. Some preachers, unfortunately, played this role so well that they neglected the development of a strong spiritual or biblical agenda.

Another role that the Black preacher has excelled in is that of prophet. The prophetic ministry of the Black preacher is established in the literature and experience of African Americans in this country. Since life was so difficult, African Americans saw the church as an oasis to hear the words and music of God, whose daily presence helped each individual, and thus the community, endure the holocaust of slavery and the oppression of an unequal society. African Americans looked to the preacher, who from the weekly forum of his pulpit gave the word needed to make it through another week. This word helped the congregants process the great disparity all around them and equipped them to apply the truth of Scripture to daily life.

The preaching (as we see in greater detail in chapter 7) came out of the experience of the preacher more often than from a book. So it connected directly with the experience of people in his congregation. Even today the preacher's primary mode of influence is the spoken word, Sunday after Sunday as he shapes the minds, wills, and emotions of his congregation.

The various roles of the Black preacher and his involvement with his people have not lessened as the Black church has become more urban in the twentieth century. Not only has he continued to have a prominent voice within the urban context, he has provided a vital link between rural traditions of the past and urban customs of major cities, such as Chicago, New York, and Detroit.

The Black preacher has always been politically involved. Because he has had a prominent position, he has felt the responsibility to use that position to influence his parishioners. Early on, the preacher in the Black church condemned colonization and segregation.

Today he is no less political, although he may not have the influence he had in the nineteenth century when his congregation was more dependent on him to interpret current events.

We have seen, however, in recent history the impact of the clergy in the leadership of the civil rights movement. It was a young Baptist minister—Martin Luther King Jr.—who led the revolution heard around the world. Chapter 8 deals further with the involvement of the church in the freedom movement.

It was another Baptist preacher who was the first Black man to run for president of the United States. Though he didn't win the election in 1984, Jesse Jackson came closer to it than anyone would have imagined. His ability to coalesce Blacks across the country is in part attributable to the respect he enjoyed as a preacher.

The Role of Women

As the dominant role of the preacher is pivotal to comprehension of the history of the Black church in America, so is the historic role—or lack of a role—of women in leadership in the Black church. Historically, women in this country have been second-class citizens. Not until women gained the right to vote did they have any role in making major policy decisions of government, business, and the church. Even after they won the vote, most leadership posts continued to be held by middle-aged White men. The leadership of the Black church was also almost exclusively in the hands of men, even though women have usually outnumbered men in membership and outworked men in charitable ministries.

In Baptist and Methodist circles, if women felt called to preach, they were not free to exercise their God-given gifts. The primary place where they had some freedom was in the Holiness/Pentecostal tradition. There women found opportunities for ministry as teachers, evangelists, and pastors. In most Black religious circles, though, this was more of an exception than the norm.

Despite the obstacles women had to face, some, like Jarena Lee, were able to fulfill God's call. After hearing Bishop Richard Allen preach one afternoon in 1804, Jarena Lee joined the African Methodist congregation in Philadelphia. Some five years later she felt the call to preach and embarked on a ministry that would take her to many African Methodist Episcopal congregations. Although Allen allowed her to speak at Mother Bethel in Philadelphia, Lee found other pulpits closed to her. The idea of women addressing mixed assemblies ran counter to prevailing attitudes and denominational rules. Jarena Lee claimed the authority of an inner spiritual experience and preached by inspiration as an itinerant revivalist. Like Amanda Smith some fifty years later and other female evangelists, healers, and preachers, Jarena Lee had to make her own way, design her own ministry, and rely on divine inspiration and authority. Today there are some churches that ordain women, but there are still some that think it improper for a woman to preach or have authority over men in religious matters.

The Black Preacher Today

In the Black church today, the preacher remains the predominant force, holding the respect and admiration of his congregation. Within the wider community, however, the role and impact of the Black preacher has declined.

There are many reasons for this and they vary from community to community, but some general trends that seem to be contributing factors are these:

The proliferation of other role models in the community from entertainment, sports, and business and their visibility through the mass media

A movement away from religion of a generation of African Americans, who no longer feel loyal to a religion or a church as their parents and grandparents did

Scandals and skepticism about clergy and the publicity of abuses perpetrated by a few[10]

Some members of the most educated generation in the history of the African American experience have rejected the traditional teaching style of the Afro-centric worship experience, which emphasizes a more prophetic style of preaching. This has always been the trend among the better-educated, upper-middle-class Blacks. Now that there are more in that socioeconomic group, the move to churches that use a more didactic, teaching style is more apparent.

There has also been subtle pressure from younger members to move away from the traditional style. Many in a congregation who are forty and under want to see a more participatory style of leadership rather than the autocratic posture that has characterized the Black preacher of the past.

Yet the Black preacher still leads his flock with more power and authority and with greater freedom to enunciate the vision and direction of the church than his White counterpart is able to exercise.

Although in the last two decades we have seen the influence of the Black pastor in the church and the community begin to wane, he is still the most influential person in the daily experience of most African Americans and he is still the dominant leader of the church.

— 6 —

Music in the Black Church
Coming Alive on Sunday

One of the most prominent features of the worship service in a Black church is the music. Music helps the worshiper relate to God in praise and draws him or her away from the cares of life into an other-worldly expression of hope and faith. The music is meant to be personal—a heartfelt utterance of personal need and trust. As such, all are expected and encouraged to participate in it. Music is not only the province of the trained musicians, but a vehicle for the entire congregation, moving them into and through the worship experience.

Throughout the drama of their experience, African Americans have maintained their distinct musical identity rooted in their African past. It was evident in the earliest spirituals sung in the slave quarters and can still be heard in the contemporary music of Black Americans. Music is another part of Black American culture that is fundamentally African in form and substance. It has a direct link to Mother Africa.

During the slave years, the saga of Black music in this country began. Ripped not only from their homeland, but from their families and support systems, these strangers to the land had to turn to each other and to their God to survive.

Critical to the development of the slave communities' solidarity was a musical form in which they all could participate. Their past was founded on a strong, culturally based oral tradition. Hildred Roach writes:

> The method of oral tradition was greatly responsible for the maintenance of the samples of African heritage which miraculously survived the centuries. Because of the . . . diversity of African languages, a process of rote teaching was instrumental in sustaining the legends and music of old Africa. Although many Africans had composed their own symbols to represent language sounds, the oral tradition was still by far the most common practice in Africa for decades, and remained the most effective method of reaching the thousands of slaves in America.[1]

The slaves survived due to their ability to transfer orally their core values. The members of the African American slave community were for the most part illiterate. They exhibited a complete dependence on oral transmission for news and communication. Because of the stringent codes that buttressed the slave system, musical expression developed as the chief means of covert communication among the slaves. For instance,

> when black slaves were not allowed to congregate or to communicate in groups, the black preacher, who had to keep his identity as a preacher concealed, devised ways of preaching to the slaves. He would tell the water boy to announce the service at a given time by singing through the fields, "Steal Away." All the slaves knew to go to the swampy forest that night for worship.[2]

Singing to communicate, to remember their past, and to comment on the present became a way of life. As they learned about the Christian God, it was natural that they would also sing about him.

But many have wondered where the songs originated. In "O Black and Unknown Bards," poet James Weldon Johnson asked, "Hear of what slave poured out such melody as 'steal away to Jesus'? Folklorist, musicologists, and historians have pondered the question of the origin of the slave spirituals. Some credited white camp meetings and revivals, others pointed to similarities with traditional African chants and praise songs." Slaves drew on Bible stories, sermons, hymns, and especially the spiritual to survive the emotional and physical rigors of slavery.[3]

The church—at this time the invisible church of the plantation—was a dominant influence in the lives of the slaves. The music they sang together gave cohesion and commonality to the slaves' experience. The shared music carried a sense of community. "If a member of the group could not sing, he could tap his foot; if he could not tap, he could sway his head; and if he could not do this, he could witness. Everyone was expected to participate."[4] The music served as an indispensable support system for the establishment, growth, and continuity of the Black church.

It is significant that the spiritual has the recurring themes of hope and confidence of liberation.

Wendel Whalum, a contemporary authority on the Afro-American Spiritual, notes that despite the Spiritual being rooted in a Black life-style that was desperately trying to cope with poor social conditions, there was never acceptance of those poor conditions because hope was always the Spiritual's central theme.[5]

Being a child of God meant hope and security. This is what the Christian slave clung to. This is what he could sing about.

It is out of this sense of being a child of God that the genius of the religious folk songs is born. There were three

85

major sources from which the raw material of the Negro Spirituals were derived: The Old and New Testaments, the world of nature, and the personal experiences of religion which were a common lot to the people, emerging from their inner life. Echoes from each source are present in practically all of the songs.[6]

Lovell, in *Black Song: The Forge and the Flame,* gives seven purposes for the spiritual:

1. To give the community a true, valid, and useful song
2. To keep the community invigorated
3. To inspire the uninspired individual
4. To enable the group to face its problems
5. To comment on the slave situation
6. To help each member gain a sense of belonging in a confusing and terrifying world
7. To provide a code language for emergency use[7]

The best estimate of the earliest appearance of the spiritual as we know it is 1760. Eventually the music of the Black religious experience, with its African imprint, became not only the root of all Black music, but of all American music. It is considered the first folk music of America. Some would say it is America's only folk music.[8]

There are two characteristics of spirituals that set them apart from other religious music: their rhythm and the antiphonal, or call-and-response, manner in which they are sung. Other characteristics include:

- Deep biblical insight. Many spiritual texts come from the Bible, particularly from the Old Testament.
- Timeless message. They still speak to human circumstances today.
- Repetitive melody. A pattern (or patterns) exists in the melodic line that repeats with slight variation.

Repetition of the lyric line or verse frequently provides a double quality of repetition.

- Unique imagery. The imagery is evocative; it reflects the painful experiences common in the slave community, such as the breaking up of the slave family on arrival in the new world, separation from the motherland, and the master's whip. The real spirituals are not just songs but songs that are built around a theme.[9]

Meter Music Supplants the Spiritual

After the Emancipation Proclamation the visible church replaced the invisible plantation church; it continued to be an institution of primary importance in the lives of Black Americans. By this time meter music, known as "Dr. Watts's music," had become popular in the churches.

In 1707 Isaac Watts, an English minister, poet, and hymn writer, published *Hymns and Spiritual Songs*. These were poems on religious themes. They were sung to familiar tunes, which made them easy for congregations to learn. These poems became especially popular during the camp meetings of the Great Awakening of the 1720s. It was at these meetings that many Blacks were first converted. The use of the Watts-style hymn, or meter music, in Black worship began between 1807 and 1810 and its development continued until about 1900. This time span covered the periods of slavery, Reconstruction, and post-Reconstruction.

Meter is the measure, or standard, by which the long and short syllables in the verses of a hymn are arranged rhythmically into groups of syllables, or poetic feet. As it applies to music, the generic term *meter* is the "basic rhythmic pattern of beats per measure, note values, and accents."[10] Meter music is characterized by the frequent repetition of lines and melody. There are various combinations of lines and syllables. The most common is the four-line stanza with

alternating lines of six and eight syllables. Here is one of
Isaac Watts's hymns in that meter:

> O God, our help in ages past,
> Our hope for years to come,
> Our shelter from the stormy blast,
> And our eternal home!

Meter music was usually sung without accompaniment.
It was often sung with the leader saying two lines of the
hymn at a time, before they were sung by the congregation. This is known as the "lining technique" and is still
used in some churches today.

What attracted slaves and former slaves to meter music?
Three factors seem to have had influence:

1. The quatrains were easy to memorize. When meter
   music was most popular, Blacks were for the most part
   illiterate. They could memorize and sing Dr. Watts's
   music.
2. More formal worship developed. In freedom, Blacks
   quickly formed their own churches, built church
   buildings, and participated in a more formal worship
   service than they had previously. The meter music
   seemed to fit with their more formal service.
3. Emancipated African Americans had a greater awareness of the larger religious community. They could
   now identify with Christians beyond their previously
   all-encompassing slave consciousness. Now that they
   were free, they would sing the music of the larger community around them.[11]

The developing Black religious community not only gave
the Watts-style hymn their unique musical imprint, but
also in their hearts they were singing to the same God of
the Spirituals who was vastly different from the God of the
slave owners and overseers. The God of the Spirituals had

delivered them from the bondage of "Egypt"; the new hymns were fashioned to suit the use of the newly freed former slaves.[12]

Here is an example:

> I love the Lord: he heard my cries,
> And pitied every groan:
> Long as I live, when troubles rise,
> I'll hasten to his throne.
>
> I love the Lord: he bowed his ear,
> And chased my grief away:
> Oh, let my heart no more despair
> While I have breath to pray.
>
> The Lord beheld me sore distressed;
> He bade my pains remove;
> Return, my soul, to God, thy rest,
> For thou hast known his love.[13]

The meter hymn did not replace the spiritual; it represented an expanding religious consciousness and changing social context that reflected the growing musical repertoire of the slave and former slave.

Anthropologists agree that the music of a people reveals much about who they are. So the Black spiritual can give us insight into the freedman, his thoughts, fears, hopes, and expectations. All that he had been through and was currently facing served as the basic elements from which the music was mined.

"It follows, then, that the variations of music sung by post-slavery Black people in this republic . . . would also be in some measure an index to their response to the changing and shifting social context."[14]

Black Baptists used the Watts hymns the most. The poems and music lent themselves to the fervent singing that has always been characteristic of Baptists.

Hymns of Improvisation

Another critical body of music that came into prominence at the beginning of the twentieth century was the "hymns of improvisation" (Wyatt Tee Walker's term). Walker says, "This body of hymns is almost entirely Euro-American in origin and authorship. With the exception of C. A. Tindley, Lucie Campbell, and a few others, not many Black poets gave themselves to hymn form in the technical sense."[15] Walker identifies two developments that encouraged the use of these hymns in the worship services of the Black community:

- Accelerated growth of the Black church as an institution.
- A sharp increase in literacy before the turn of the century. As Blacks became more educated, hymns that better fit their cultural perspective became more accepted in the Black community.

To these developments I would add a third that greatly influenced the use of hymns of improvisation: the movement of Blacks to the urban centers. This movement exchanged the previously rural posture of the Black religious experience for one that was more reflective of the process of urbanization. As the Black community became increasingly urban, churches began to adopt more Euro-American hymns. In the twentieth century, Black churches were taking on an urban look. They became larger in size and more impressive in structure, increasingly patterning their worship after the dominant community. After building larger church buildings in the 1920s, 1930s, and 1940s, they began to feel the need for pianos and organs.

During this stage the Euro-American hymn came into broad use in the Black church. The hymnal was introduced into Black worship, but not everyone was literate. Thus,

the choir led the congregation in hymns with enough repetition that those who were not yet able to read could learn
the words and sing along. Choirs and choir directors became an integral part of the worship service.

Gospel Music

As we have seen, African American sacred music began
with the creation of the spiritual. Meter music and Euro-
American hymns were later incorporated into the worship service, but the Black spiritual form influenced their
use. These musical forms from the dominant community
were adapted to suit the religious needs of the Black
community.

"Gospel music, in the words of Tony Heilbut, 'good news
and bad times,' was spawned in the midst of the nation's
worst economic crisis. The Gospel form evidenced the
blues-jazz mode from the so-called secular world and re-
joined old roots almost forgotten."[16] Thomas A. Dorsey,
the father of gospel music, gave the music its name.

Gospel music came into being during the depression
years. Wyatt Tee Walker writes, "Gospel music, at bottom,
is religious folk music that is clearly identifiable with the
social circumstance of the Black community in America."[17]

Dorsey made a similar statement during a 1974 interview: "Somebody once wrote that I see gospel music 'as
meaning a message of good tidings expounded by one who
has walked the path of trouble and hard times.'"[18]

The authenticity of folk ways and folk expressions, including music, can be gauged by how closely they mirror
the experience of the group they represent. If this is true,
gospel music's authenticity as the music of an oppressed
people during an oppressive time (the Great Depression)
cannot be challenged. As has been shown throughout history, when there is upheaval in a nation, it generally affects the poor and downtrodden even more than the gen-

91

eral population. Gospel music in the midst of the pain of economic, political, and social poverty has given Black people hope for a better day when Jesus would come back. Gospel music is not only a reflection of difficult times but a testimony of triumphant faith.

Shortly before World War I a steady migration of southern Blacks to the urban areas of the North began. The movement escalated after the war and was so widespread that it has come to be called the Great Migration. Blacks were in search of greater economic opportunities, and jobs in northern cities were an irresistible attraction.

The southern migrants brought with them religious traditions that found an outlet for expression in humble storefronts and small church buildings.

Life in the northern ghetto was dismal. It was an unfamiliar life with none of the familiar trappings of the South. The support system of neighbors and friends had been left behind. The cities became less and less hospitable as segregation policies were put in place. Life was hard, and gospel music arrived on the scene just in time to ease the pain a little.

The Development of Gospel Music

Early in the twentieth century Charles Albert Tindley was attempting to interpret the hardships of ghetto life through his music. He wrote songs that would serve as vehicles of survival and this made them different, more meaningful and accessible than the music that had come before. His "new music" gained popularity as he gave concerts at his church in Philadelphia. Tindley wrote such favorites as "Some Day," "He'll Understand and Say Well Done," and "I'll Overcome Someday," which was later adapted as the anthem of the civil rights movement.

Religious music was reflecting the feelings and difficulties of the times.

Wendel Whalum notes this parallel: "The first three decades of the century also saw the shift in the world of secular music, from ragtime to blues, to the recording of the blues, and the introduction of jazz. In no small measure did these expressions have their effect on gospel music. In fact one of the leaders in the gospel music movement, Thomas A. Dorsey, was active as a blues pianist and, before 1919, had been one of the successful pianists in the South."[19]

Thomas Dorsey turned to writing and arranging religious music after a serious illness in the mid–1920s. His genius was that he seemed to capture in his music the very soul of an oppressed people and gave them hope. This shows the influence of C. A. Tindley's music on Dorsey.

Thomas Dorsey is considered the father of gospel music and his impact on the development of this genre lasted from 1930 to 1945. Dorsey was the first to write gospel songs and tirelessly promoted the music. In 1932 Dorsey and Sallie Martin organized the first Black gospel music convention, the National Convention of Gospel Choirs and Choruses.

Through the years Dorsey's music touched hundreds of gospel singers, such as Mahalia Jackson and Lillian Bowles. Other gospel composers, such as Lucie Campbell and Kenneth Morris, also helped to popularize gospel music. As America moved closer to World War II, gospel music became more entrenched as part of the Black church experience.

So large did Dorsey's influence loom over the gospel music world, that much of the music of that era was referred to as "Dorsey's." Everyone was into gospel; Blacks and Whites hailed it as the lifeblood of American religious music.

In the 1940s such groups as the Dixie Hummingbirds, the Golden Gate, and the Charioteers became popular. In the early 1950s some gospel groups were commanding four-figure guarantees, and many were making recordings. The groups and individuals performing gospel music during the

1940s and 1950s had a profound influence on the genre's development. This is true of each era as the music has evolved. It has continued to meet the needs of performer and audience, interpreting the current state of affairs and offering hope for survival.

Modern gospel, as sung by such artists as the Winans, Babbie Mason, and Andraé Crouch, maintains the traditional emphasis of an upward focus on heaven and God's ability to overcome adversity with a more upbeat style. In the last several years the gospel sound has become not only big business but also greatly diversified. The advent of advanced technology has brought gospel into everyone's home, and the distinctions between the secular and the sacred are disappearing.

Music in the Black church maintains its cultural distinctives but is becoming more and more varied. Contemporary praise and worship choruses out of the Maranatha movement have found their way into many Black churches, but most continue to rely on the gospel tradition.

—7—

Preaching
in the Black Church

In his book *Are Blacks Spiritually Inferior to Whites?*, Tony Evans writes, "In the Black religious experience, preaching is much more than one man sharing the Word with the congregation. Preaching is an event."[1] As an African American minister of the gospel, I have experienced firsthand the truth of Dr. Evans's statement. It is the most consuming passion of those called to preach within the African American context.

Henry Mitchell, noted homiletician and scholar, reinforces this point when he writes,

> The preaching tradition of the Black Fathers did not spring into existence suddenly. It was developed after a long and often quite disconnected series of contacts between the Christian gospel variously interpreted and men caught up in the Black experience of slavery and oppression. To this experience and this gospel they brought their own culture and folkways. . . . Very prominent in that Black religious tradition were black-culture sermons and the way Black men delivered and responded to them.[2]

Mitchell, in his description of the centrality of preaching within the African American context, makes a point we need to examine in more detail. He says it was out of the context of slavery and oppression that the gospel was interpreted and proclaimed. He also says that the early spirituals, a form of sermonic solo, laid the foundation for the significance of preaching. These sung sermons gave those under abysmal conditions a sense of hope.

Not only was preaching central in the life of a Black church because it inspired hope, but, as we have seen, it emerged within the context of a culture that has a strong oral tradition as its primary method of disseminating information, the roots of this phenomenon being in its African past.

J. Deotis Roberts, in his book A *Black Political Theology*, writes: "There is continuity as well as discontinuity between the African past of Black Americans and their present situation. Black American culture is synthetic. We have to deal with a cultural duality. We do not remember our past and until rather recently many Black Americans had no desire to remember their African antecedents."[3] But the oral tradition of the elders gave Blacks dignity, heritage, and hope, reminding them that adversity had been overcome in their African past.

This comfort with oral tradition laid the foundation for the sermon being central to the worship experience of the African American. The varied and small gathering that was part of developing the invisible institution of the Black church allowed for the emergence of the Black preacher as central disseminator of truth. He was the one who could relate the past and the present to God.

The Black preacher isn't trained to preach. He learns his craft through observing others, and then doing it himself. By the time he delivers his first sermon, he has participated in the worship event and has heard the preacher's varied intonations, seen his expansive gestures, been caught up in the call and response. Preaching isn't just something a man can do; it's something he can feel.

Preaching was, and still is, a combination of biblical storytelling and doctrinal exegesis. The Black preacher paints pictures to make biblical truths come alive for his audience. The imagination of both preacher and congregation is used to move the worship experience from simply the delivery of information to a celebration of praise to God.

It is often true that African Americans who receive formal seminary training lose some of their ability to preach to a predominately Black audience. If not careful, they can come out of seminary with all the right exegetical and hermeneutical tools but be unable to relate culturally or to be relevant to their congregations. Their education may have reduced the preaching task to an academic exercise.[4] This process is encouraged in many conservative evangelical seminaries that teach the "right way to preach" is the "White way."

On the other hand, there is a danger of equating good preaching with Black preaching and allowing emotionalism to replace exegesis. Black preaching is good when it not only gets the congregation involved, but raises their awareness of God and his claim on their lives.

Dialogical Preaching

One of the first things a person from another culture will notice when entering the typical Black Baptist church is the dialogue that takes place between preacher and parishioner. This call-and-response pattern in preaching is unique to the African American religious experience.

Sermons are not unilateral but bilateral. The core of the sermon experience relates to the interaction (within the context of the sermon) of preacher and audience. This model of ministry, although foreign to the majority community within the American evangelical church, is more reflective of the synagogue experience of the Jewish faith. The synagogue, not the temple, served as the primary place of corporate interaction on religious matters, with a dialogue process being the primary mode of information dissemination.

Components of Dialogical Preaching

Let's look at the critical components of dialogical preaching that distinguish it from the traditional monological mode of the majority community.

Dialogical preaching follows the call-and-response pattern. It is essentially a continuing dialogue between the preacher and congregation. As such, it is much more interactive than the typical sermon given as a monologue. The preacher of a monologue sermon may occasionally receive a response from the audience—an "amen" or a laugh. He may on occasion ask for a response, perhaps an answer to a question, but he doesn't expect or even want the dialogue to continue. In the interactive style, however, the dialogue is an integral part of the sermon. It moves the preacher along and it keeps the audience involved.

Dialogical preaching tends to be spontaneous. The preacher has freedom to do whatever he wants to do to convey the message of the sermon. The response of the congregation encourages his spontaneity.

Dialogical preaching feeds off its audience. Mitchell verifies this when he writes:

> Black preaching has been shaped by interaction with the listeners. If the Black preaching tradition is unique at all, then that uniqueness depends significantly upon the uniqueness of the Black congregation, which talks back to the preacher as a normal part of the pattern of worship. By many outside the culture, the dialogue between preacher and congregation has been viewed, at best, as a quaint over-

reaction of simple folk, as exuberant expression of a beautiful, childlike faith such as could never occur in sophisticated Christian worship.[5]

In my experience the adrenaline hardly gets going until, in the middle of the homily, a parishioner says, "Come on now, Dwight, bring it." I might respond spontaneously, "Thank you, Brother," thus taking my communication to a different level of clarity and power.

Dialogical preaching is relational. Of all the characteristics of dialogical preaching, this one is most meaningful to me. I view ministry as relational in nature. Out of my relationship with God I relate to others. This relational aspect of ministry is one of the historic strengths of the Black church and the Black preacher. The preacher serves not only as communicator on Sunday morning, but as the father, brother, and comforter of his congregation throughout the week. This close relationship means that the preacher can identify with his audience. He knows what they're going through. He shares in their joys and sorrows and, after finding strength to meet his own needs, can share strength through the practical insights of the preached message. This relational aspect of dialogical preaching has always kept me in love with the style and given focus and meaning to my preaching.

Dialogical preaching clarifies truth. Part of the effectiveness of the Jewish synagogue experience, where dialogue with the speaker is expected, is the immediate interaction with the preached text. This interaction helps bring clarity. Dialogical preaching does the same. In this style, repetition is expected, so the preacher will repeat a key phrase over and over. This, and the audience participation in it, drives home and clarifies the point.

Dialogical preaching is life-application oriented. This style of preaching is not an intellectual or theological exercise. It is practical, dealing with themes of survival, especially out of the Black experience as an oppressed people.

The Black Preaching Style

From the beginning Black preaching has been characterized by an emphasis on personal style. Some homileticians would say style is of little importance when compared to the theological content of the message. It's true that all good preaching must have, at its foundation, strong and accurate exegesis. Style and presentation, however, make a congregation listen to a preacher week after week.

There are some aspects of style that are basic to Black preaching:

- *Unusual mannerisms.* These are more acceptable in the Black church context than in the majority community. In many White churches, for example, it would be unacceptable for a preacher to leave the pulpit and walk up and down the aisle. In most Black churches, though, this is expected.
- *Sustained tone.* Some have called it "whooping." Preachers use this musical chant or tone for different effects. Some use it to emphasize the climax of the message, while others use it throughout the message.
- *Rhythm.* The pace of the delivery and its rhythm help draw the audience into the message.
- *Call and response.* We have already discussed this aspect, the central dynamic of Black preaching.
- *Repetition.* Black preachers use repetition of aphorisms and other significant statements for emphasis, memory, and effect.
- *Dramatization.* It is not unusual for a Black preacher to assume the role of a biblical character while in the pulpit.
- *Familiar phrases.* The Black preacher often has a repertoire of short, easily remembered phrases that he uses in his sermons. In some cases the congregation be-

comes so familiar with them that they are able to say them along with the preacher.

- *Slow rate of delivery (at least initially)*. The fundamental significance of the slow rate of delivery is its impact. America's great Black preachers frequently develop clever, pithy statements that capture the main point of a sermon. These they deliver slowly and may repeat several times.[6]

The preaching style in a Black church may be very different from that in a White church. But each is valid and each makes an important contribution to the body as a whole. Paul wrote about this in 1 Corinthians 12, where he said that the parts of the body are different but each part is invaluable to the whole. The Black style of worship is part of God's sovereign, diversity-packed plan for his church.

The Black worship service, including the Black preaching style, makes up only one aspect of Black culture, but it is an important aspect because it is based on a heritage that goes back to Africa and is part of an institution that is unique to African Americans.

8

From Pulpit to Prison

The Civil Rights Era

I have a dream my four little children will one day live
in a nation where they will not be judged by the color of
their skin but by the content of their character. I have a
dream today.

Dr. Martin Luther King Jr.
at the Washington Monument, 1963

No other man in the past one hundred years has had as
profound an impact on the social and moral fabric of
American society as Martin Luther King Jr. African Americans who grew up in the 1950s and 1960s looked to him
as a shining light in the midst of the darkness of an American society that even to this day judges men and women
more on the color of their skin than on the content of their
character. His influence offered young African Americans
self-worth and hope in the midst of the pain that surrounded
them. Dr. Martin Luther King Jr. was adored by his fol-

lowers but hated by many others because he dared to con-
front a generation's conscience.

It has been more than forty years since the civil rights
movement was officially initiated with Mrs. Rosa Parks's
assertion of her rights as a human being and the resulting
Montgomery bus boycott of 1956. This series of events pro-
jected Dr. King to national prominence. The constant fact
demonstrated through these many years has been the cat-
alytic role that the Black church has played in the un-
shackling of a group of people.

Until 1956 the United States was for all practical purposes—especially in the South—two nations. Andrew
Hacker in his book *Two Nations* writes that this was nowhere more evident than in the South, which had refused
to acknowledge that there was ever an end to the Civil
War or that something called the Emancipation Proclamation existed. Thus the South continued to keep Blacks—
regardless of their abilities, skill, or background—in literal
bondage through the oppressive laws of segregation and
the dehumanizing customs of Jim Crowism.

One law required Blacks in some areas of the South to
sit in the back of a bus in the "Colored people section"
(even when there were plenty of seats in the front). It was
the inhumanity of this law and others like it that ignited
the Montgomery bus boycott. Ralph Abernathy, in his autobiography *And the Walls Came Tumbling Down*, writes of
this event:

> Most accounts of the Montgomery bus boycott begin with
> the refusal of Rosa Parks to obey a bus driver's order. As a
> matter of fact, two black women had already been arrested
> earlier in the year. One of them, Claudette Colvin, a fif-
> teen-year-old student, had been dragged from the bus and
> charged with assault and battery as well as failure to com-
> ply with Jim Crow laws governing public transportation.
> In each of these earlier cases, Mrs. Jo Ann Robinson, a pro-

fessor of English at Alabama State University, had represented the defendants in negotiations with bus officials and city fathers, hoping to put an end to such incidents before they resulted in violence.

Mrs. Robinson, who headed an activist group called Women's Political Council, had invited black pastors to join her in confronting the white establishment, if only to emphasize the point that our entire community was disturbed by what was happening. At that time, few of the other clergy were concerned with questions of social justice and Martin [Luther King] was too preoccupied with finishing his dissertation, so I was the only one who had accepted her invitation. . . .

At these meetings, we discussed not only the two women who had been arrested, but also a number of additional bus incidents. . . . We tried to reason with local authorities and with bus company officials. They were polite, listened to our complaints with serious expressions on their faces, and did nothing.[1]

With this as background, "On December 1, 1955, Mrs. Parks took her now-famous bus ride and set events in motion. . . ." The civil rights movement was about to begin. "A seamstress at a large department store, [Mrs. Parks] was a slight woman, soft-spoken and courteous."[2] There is no evidence that it was her intention to become the symbol of a social revolution that would shake the country.

Out of this context rose a new organization, the church-based Southern Christian Leadership Conference (SCLC). The Rev. Dr. Martin Luther King Jr. became president. Launched to bring real freedom and a better life to all Black people, the movement was rooted in the church and in the Christian principles of love and brotherhood. Just as had ancient Israel, SCLC saw God as the deliverer of his oppressed people. SCLC also adopted the nonviolent principles that Mahatma Gandhi had used in India. Dr. King used this nonviolent approach for the boycott in Montgomery and then across the country. His message of nonviolence and brotherhood became the backbone of the early part of the civil rights struggle. This approach required hours and hours of training on the local level, with emphasis on biblical principles. It was an approach that related to a theology of suffering and meekness, and the example of Christ's sufferings was constantly emphasized.

This nonviolent worldview has its roots in the days of slavery and the beginnings of the Black church in America. It remains crucial to the survival of a people once oppressed by the inhumane conditions of legal (before 1865) oppression and people who are now frequently the objects of oppression because of racial prejudice against them.

The Role of the Church

It was the clergy and church members who mobilized the civil rights movement. The church served as the central hub and command center for protests and marches because, in the 1950s and 1960s, the church was still the central institution of the Black community. In some areas during this era, the preacher was the most prominent person in the community. The church was the only organization where Blacks had ownership and control. Thus the church—whether in small communities of the South or in urban centers in the North—was the beachhead for this fledgling movement. And because the movement rose from the church, it was spiritual in nature, a sacred quest.

This was no more evident than in the Montgomery bus boycott that became a model for future civil rights intervention. Abernathy recalls a conversation he had with E. D. Nixon when they were trying to decide how to respond to Mrs. Parks's arrest. They immediately thought of getting the church involved. Abernathy is speaking:

"I believe we should ask Dr. Hubbard to call a meeting of
black leaders under the auspices of the Baptist Ministers
Conference. He's probably the most highly respected cler-
gyman in the black community. If anyone can speak with
authority to both races, it's Dr. Hubbard."

Nixon was hesitant. He didn't think Dr. Hubbard was
dynamic enough, even though he was his own pastor. But
I knew that Hubbard was well loved in the community, so
I pressed the matter. . . .

Of course, I knew that the Baptists alone could not act
in behalf of the entire community so as soon as I contacted
the last member of our Conference, I began to call the
Methodist clergy, . . . but I couldn't find any of them at
their churches, and when I tried at home I had the same
luck. Finally, one pastor's wife told me why: the AME Zion-
ists were gathering that morning at Hilliard Chapel AME
Zion Church to meet with their bishop. Since they were
by far the largest group of black clergy outside the Baptists,
I decided to go speak to them all at once.[3]

Not only did the Black church fill the role of command
center for the movement, but it was a training center as
well. Much of the training for the nonviolent approach to
civil disobedience of Dr. King and the SCLC was done in
churches. Churches throughout the South also housed civil
rights demonstrators who came in from the North; church
folk risked their lives to care for these demonstrators. The
church generated and funneled through its doors the resources necessary to mobilize communities. This centrality of distribution continues today, as the Black church is
the corporate entity richest in the resources that Black people control.

Here are just a few examples of what is being done today:
The housing initiatives of Antioch Baptist Church on the
southside of Chicago have literally transformed part of that
beleaguered community. Deliverance Church of God in
Christ in Philadelphia has a massive community economic

development program in the inner city. West Angeles Church of God in Christ in Los Angeles with its ministries in the areas of education, housing, and community economic development are bringing hope to literally thousands of inner-city residents.

During the civil rights movement the church also served as an inspiration center. People gathered regularly at churches to hear messages of encouragement and hope from their leaders. The Sunday sermon often centered on the ideals of the movement as just and God-honoring. Again it was the Black preacher who was catapulted to the forefront of the movement because he was in a prominent leadership position and because he could provide inspiration to carry on.

While the Black church played such a mighty role in the civil rights movement, the conservative, evangelical White church's lack of involvement (often to the point of antagonism) is painfully evident. Liberal denominations and churches demonstrated more commitment and a greater involvement than the "Bible-believing evangelicals." This neglect bordered on racism in some quarters. Some purportedly evangelical schools even propagated racist teachings related to the inferiority of African Americans. They asserted that Black churches preached a "social" gospel and that Martin Luther King was a communist.

King's Leadership

Martin Luther King, in his position as undisputed leader of the civil rights movement, was bound to draw the ire of those opposed to his crusade. But he felt God's call to be in the forefront, inspiring his followers despite the attention, and therefore the risks, entailed.

Martin Luther King was, above all, a preacher. He possessed great oratory style and the enviable ability to paint pictures with his words, clarifying abstract and difficult-to-grasp concepts. This gift was crucial in preaching freedom to a people who had known only oppression and discrimination.

There were other reasons for Dr. King's becoming such a monumental figure in the history of African Americans and American society in general. He was a man of destiny. He was in the right place at the right time. After years of oppression, the time was right for Blacks to ask for their God-given rights and King was there to lead the way. He was the epitome of a visionary, transformational leader, who was able to mobilize the vision and dreams of a generation. People loved to listen to him and were willing to follow his lead because of his own unwavering commitment to the cause of equality for all people. He loved *all* people and sought justice for all. His love for people did not stop with those of his own race.

March on Washington

Most scholars consider the pinnacle of the civil rights movement to be the 1963 March on Washington. More than 250,000 people gathered in Washington under the leadership of Dr. King to demonstrate their desire for equality of economic opportunity. People of all races from across the country came to Washington to show their support of the movement and to express their desire for change. At this event Dr. King gave his most memorable speech: "I Have a Dream."

Like other crucial events in the history of African Americans, the church provided leadership, resources, and organizational energy to make the March on Washington possible. After this event, though, the nonviolent movement led by Dr. King began to lose momentum. The proliferation of other civil rights groups with divergent views emerged, with the focus shifting away from Dr. King. There were those who disagreed strongly with King and his philosophy of nonviolence, such as Stokely Carmichael of the

Student Nonviolent Coordinating Committee (SNCC), Huey Newton of the Black Panther Party, and Malcolm X. These people caught the imaginations of younger urban African Americans.

Even within King's camp, subtle divisions existed. His associates became polarized, with the older ones siding with Ralph Abernathy and the younger ones loyal to Jesse Jackson. This division was under control as long as King was alive; however, after King died, Jesse Jackson left the Southern Christian Leadership Conference and formed his own civil rights organization, Operation Push.

As the decade of the 1960s progressed, the focus of many Americans was changing from the civil rights movement to the war in Vietnam. Even Dr. King, toward the end of his life, was revising his message. He had been seeking long-term change through legislation and politics but began to see the need to develop an economic base that could empower his people. Unfortunately he had just begun that phase of his crusade when, on April 4, 1968, he was assassinated. He was in Memphis to provide leadership for the sanitation workers' strike there. Many felt not only sadness and pain, but resentment and anger that one so great and so young (Dr. King was only thirty-nine) had been taken away.

9

A New Wave

The Emergence of the Black Evangelical

Much of the literature written in the last one hundred years regarding the Black church has approached the topic primarily from the perspective of the historic Black church. This is not surprising since the majority of African Americans in this country (70–75 percent, based on published denominational figures) belong to the seven historic Black denominations.

In the last thirty years, however, there has been a growing segment of Black religious life that is part of the conservative evangelical branch of the church. This is happening within the established Black church and as a new movement of Black evangelicals.

Recently we have seen a resurgence, a spiritual renewal, of many historic Black congregations that had been mired in traditionalism and even liberalism in relationship to the fundamental doctrines of orthodox Christianity. These congregations are led by men and women (predominately men) whom I would classify as neo-evangelical.

There is also a significant group of African Americans that participates in predominately White mainline Protestant denominations such as Lutheran, Episcopal, and Presbyterian, as well as the Roman Catholic Church. It is difficult to come up with an accurate figure, but a rough estimate is that between 10 and 20 percent of African American parishioners are in these denominations.

Historic Black Church

The historic Black church, as we have seen, is distinctive in several areas.

It is Black-led. The historic Black church was the first institution, and for two hundred or more years the only institution, led and controlled by African Americans. It was the only institution where the leadership of a Black man was sought and embraced. In the rest of society he was looked down on and denied leadership—even in his home.

It teaches a holistic gospel. The historic Black church never had the option of dichotomizing the gospel. Unlike the majority community that could spend hours discussing the validity and the necessity of the "social gospel," the historic Black church had no such luxury. The gospel was relevant only as it offered physical and emotional freedom, along with spiritual freedom, to its adherents.

It serves as a community center. The historic Black church was the communication, distribution, and inspiration center of the Black community. Up until the last fifteen to twenty years the church was the main source of information for Black people.

Its preaching is unique. Dialogical preaching, the call-and-response format, comprised the final authoritative word not just in spiritual matters but in all matters of life. The preacher (not the news broadcaster, as it is today) was the interpreter of the times for his parishioners.

Its worship is heartfelt. Worship in the historic Black church evolved out of an ethos of slavery and sought to bring hope that was heavenward and earthbound.

Denominationalism is important. As denominations developed and matured, control, power, and self-esteem spread from the local church body to the broader denomination. Denominationalism became an identity badge that traveled with the worshipers as they moved from one community to the next.

Evangelical Movement

Jesus reminds his listeners in Matthew 9:17 that you cannot put new wine in old wineskins. A new skin must be used for new wine. Within the Black church today there is a movement (Black evangelicalism) seeking to put new wine in old skins. This movement seeks to bring evangelicalism into the mainstream experience of Black people.

In the early 1960s young Black men and women, many of whom had grown up in the historic Black church, came into contact with training systems (the conservative Bible college, Christian college, and, to a lesser degree, the White seminary) and ministry systems (White parachurch movements, such as Campus Crusade for Christ and The Navigators). These contacts caused their worldview to be influenced by Euro-American values and their religion to be affected by conservative evangelical worship and beliefs.

I know intimately this conservative, evangelical wing of the church. As a young adult in the early 1970s, I came to know Christ through a parachurch ministry. As a result of this contact, my perception of my culture was altered. Also my theology was now filtered through a grid that reinforced middle-class White values. In looking back, I realize that this early influence was beneficial to my spiritual development but it certainly hindered my ability to connect with my own community.

113

Attracting Youth

InterVarsity Christian Fellowship, The Navigators, Campus Crusade for Christ, and other similar parachurch organizations originated during the 1930s, 1940s, and 1950s in response to some churches' perceptions that they were being ineffective in evangelism and equipping of leadership. Primarily White middle class in origin, these movements came into contact with African Americans on college campuses in the 1960s and 1970s. These young people had rejected the historic, traditional Black church due to the perception that it was irrelevant and at times hypercritical and were looking for an alternative religious tradition.

The groups were effective in relating to young African Americans. They offered a sound theological subsystem (true to conservative, orthodox Christianity) and used sophisticated ministry skills in evangelism and discipleship. However, they also transferred bias against Black worship style and misunderstanding of the validity and credibility of the African American religious tradition.

Partially as a result of the parachurch ministry on college and high school campuses, many young Blacks began to seek educational experiences consistent with their newfound understanding of religion. Some turned for training to such schools as Dallas Theological Seminary, Trinity Evangelical Divinity School, and Moody Bible Institute. These schools had a profound impact on the theological constructs that many of these emerging leaders would develop. The distinct evangelical subculture of these institutions profoundly affected many of these aspiring leaders.

Distinctives of the Evangelical Church

Formal training is expected. The leadership and laity emphasize formal training as part of the qualification for ministry. No longer is it acceptable to be called to the ministry and receive one's primary training within a lay or mentor-

114

ing context from other preachers. This has positive and negative aspects.

On the positive side, this is an acknowledgment of the need to upgrade the skills and knowledge base of the ministry profession in an age of increased specialization. This is possible for a generation (the first in the history of African Americans) with unparalleled access to higher education.

On the negative side, many seminaries and Bible colleges have historically emphasized the pursuit of academic credentials to the neglect of the need for strong mentoring from someone in ministry. This tends to develop ministers whose conceptual abilities outweigh their experience.

Its worship style is unique. The worship of the Black evangelical church integrates the historic African American worship style with contemporary gospel and praise. Worship distinctives—such as call-and-response preaching, highly emotive worship, and expressive forms of music—are maintained, yet those that tend to be primarily associated with the Black church, such as emotionalism, are de-emphasized.

Church planting is an integral part. In the traditional Black church, new churches were started primarily as a result of church splits or divisions. In the evangelical church movement there is an emphasis on evangelism and missions; outreach to the community through parent/daughter–church relationships is an important part of ministry.

Salvation is emphasized. In the evangelical Black church a personal conversion as the prime prerequisite for salvation is acknowledged. Church membership and baptism, especially as they relate to one's salvation experience, are not considered equal to but rather subsequent evidences of one's personal conversion experience. This is different from the traditional church in which there is often little differentiation between church membership and a conversion experience.

It has adopted a conservative agenda. The evangelical Black church tends to be more conservative than its traditional counterpart. This conservatism is not just theological but political as well. The evangelical Black church is not as committed to a social justice agenda as the historic Black church has been.

Its preaching is expository. Expository preaching, in which the meaning of a Scripture text is explained, is the usual preaching style. This differs from the preaching in the traditional church, which tends to be more topical and thematic, emphasizing the "telling of the story."

Denominational affiliation is not considered important. The evangelical movement de-emphasizes denominational affiliation. Many evangelical Black churches are a part of the independent Bible church movement begun in the early 1960s by Dr. Ruben Conner, of the Dallas-based Urban Evangelical Mission. Others are part of the Plymouth Brethren movement that de-emphasizes denominational ties.

Lay training is emphasized. Lay workers often participate in various White conservative training systems. Sunday school conventions and Christian conferences on evangelism by such groups as Campus Crusade have drawn greater numbers from the ranks of African American evangelicals than the historic Black church.

Neo-Evangelical Church

The third major segment of the current Black church movement in America is the neo-evangelical movement. This movement is growing at a fast pace, making a larger impact than the evangelical Black church movement, which I predict will remain rather small due to its narrower lifestyle and theological commitments.

The following are some distinctives of the neo-evangelical movement.

It has historic roots. Black neo-evangelicals have not abandoned their historic Black church roots. Unlike the evangelical Black Church movement, which has created new evangelical churches, neo-evangelical laypeople and clergy continue to worship in the context of the seven historic Black denominations.

There is an emphasis on an educated clergy. This group's leaders are men and women between the ages of thirty and forty-five, who have had some formal higher education. The education is typically undergraduate work at a secular university rather than formal seminary training. They consider formal education as a prerequisite for effective ministry, even though this does not necessarily mean formal training at an accredited Bible college or seminary. They also recognize the importance and value of exposure to traditional Black training systems, such as through mentors and learning the ministry by doing.

Worship tends to be traditional. They affirm as relevant and effective the traditional worship expression. However, they would be more diverse in their worship repertoire than the historic Black church by including contemporary praise and gospel songs.

The preaching is expository. This is the desired mode of communication from the pulpit on Sunday morning, although dialogical preaching is also used on a somewhat regular basis. Teaching and training are emphasized rather than preaching, and the members are encouraged to do Bible study. Salvation is emphasized rather than just church membership.

White Mainline Denominational Groups

The fourth segment of the African American church is comprised of those churches and individuals who worship within predominately White mainline traditions. Compared to the other three segments of the Black church, this

117

group is not as visible in the Black community. Yet its numbers are significant. Blacks involved in these traditions either develop their own identity, separate from the White church, or they are so amalgamated into the White tradition that the Black community does not perceive them as having a significant power base.

The following are distinctives of the White mainline denominational Black church.

Their economic status is distinctive. Most Blacks in these movements tend to be middle- or upper-middle-class.

There is an emphasis on clergy education. These churches expect their clergy to be properly educated. Many of the seminaries affiliated with the more liberal denominations have been aggressive in seeking students among people of color and women. Thus, these denominations have been able to create a niche for African American leaders that has led to the establishment of Black churches of these denominations.

There is often a liberal view of salvation. In these churches, social and political action often intermingle with one's view of salvation. Often, as a result of a more liberal view of Scripture, salvation is equated with works. Empowerment issues and political and social renewal receive high priority. Dogma and tradition are as important as Scripture in the evaluation of one's faith and practice.

The worship style follows the White tradition. Often there is a prescribed liturgy and this is central to the worship experience.

Racism and the Evangelical Church

Just as there are distinct segments of the Black church in this country, so are there segments of the White church (isn't it sad we have to accept nomenclature that is antibiblical?). The White church is divided along theological and socio-cultural issues. In the late nineteenth and early twentieth centuries, the fundamentalist movement began in response to the turning of many theological training centers toward a liberal neo-orthodox view of Scripture (this view tends to de-emphasize inerrancy and gravitate toward an allegorical instead of literalist view of the interpretation of Scripture). This movement gained steam with the development of the Bible college movement in this country. It dominated American thought during such test situations as the John T. Scopes trial in 1925 that focused on the evolution-versus-creation argument. During the 1930s, 1940s, and 1950s the conservative parachurch movement was influential. The fundamentalism movement is rooted even today in the basin of the so-called "Southern Bible Belt."

The fundamentalist church and the evangelical church for the most part have failed to reach out to the Black community. They have failed to share leadership of their institutions with African Americans, and their places of higher learning have been insensitive to the need of Blacks to be trained within their own context.[1] They have also failed to publish from an African American perspective literature in the biblical, popular, and theological disciplines. And often in the White fundamentalist or evangelical church there are signs of institutional racism and sometimes outright bigotry. As an African American who has walked and studied in the world of the Black church as well as in that of the White church, I can say unequivocally that, although fundamentalist and evangelical segments of the church hold to (for the most part) correct theology, they have had the wrong sociology.

In writing this chapter I risk alienating a major segment of people I intend this book to reach and help. I don't want this to happen but I must deal with this systemic issue of institutional racism, which has been well-documented among leaders in the African American and White communities.[2]

119

Before we move on, let's clarify the underlying concepts of institutional racism, covert racism, and prejudice. Institutional racism is the unintentional but real exclusion of a certain segment of the population from the benefits of an organization simply based on judgments about race. This type of racism is so embedded in an organization's operations that the exclusion is never seen as intentional, and often not noticed at all by the majority culture. It is very real, however, in the outworking of a monocultural agenda throughout an organization that is exclusive instead of inclusive. This is seen in the low level of participation of minority persons in senior positions of authority and when policies that affect Black people are made by White people without any input from the minority group.

Covert racism is intentional acts of racism that are veiled, so as to appear unintentional. This racism is often engaged in today by people who are racist but are also aware of what is considered acceptable in polite society. Covert racism may be exhibited when a salesperson follows a Black customer around in his store or tougher standards are set for Black students than for White students.

Joseph Barndt in his book *Dismantling Racism* says, "Racism goes beyond prejudice. It is backed up by power. Racism is the power to enforce one's prejudices."[3] Racism has affected all segments of the Black church, including those that have remained in White mainline denominations. For example, overt racism was the primary reason four of the seven historic denominations split from their White parent denominations. Issues such as polity, church discipline, even theology remained essentially the same as those of the White Baptist and Methodist groups. The only reason for these splits was race.

As a part of the evangelical segment of the Black church, I have felt the devastation of covert and institutional racism. It affects governance and interpretation of Scripture, among other things. Another example of racism is in my own de-nomination. A leading lay person says there is no way he could ever approve of interracial marriage. He bases his stand on an unbiblical but volatile interpretation of Scrip-ture (a belief he embraced during his years as an under-graduate student at a leading fundamentalist Christian col-lege that continues to teach as truth this unfortunate error based on a faulty interpretation of Scripture).

Institutional, covert, and overt racism have all had a hand in the estrangement of many Black and White Chris-tians. This has resulted in the continuing separation of our churches.

National Black Evangelical Association

Out of this context of pain (that consisted of more out-ward than institutional acts of racism by White conserva-tive evangelical organizations and churches), the National Black Evangelical Association was born in 1963.

A division had occurred between the National Associ-ation of Evangelicals and some of its Black participants, who felt at their wit's end concerning the racism they were experiencing. Twenty-three people from across the coun-try met in Los Angeles. Some of these individuals were serving in White parachurch, educational, and other mis-sion settings. Others were ministering in predominately Black churches and missions. According to Dr. Ruth Bent-ley, one of the original twenty-three who met in Los An-geles and whose husband, the late Dr. Bill Bentley, is con-sidered the "father of NBEA," their purpose was to provide a vehicle for the patriarchs of the emerging conservative evangelical wing of the Black church to meet annually.[4]

As it grew, the NBEA became the major forum for emerging leadership, men and women of the Institute of Black Family Development such as Matthew Parker; Ruth Bentley, formerly with InterVarsity and now a professor at the University of Illinois Circle campus; Tony Evans of Urban Alternative; and Crawford Loritts of Campus Crusade for Christ. These people were catapulted into the national evangelical spotlight.

Rev. Russell Knight, president of CURE—a national church-consulting agency—and the first African American field staff member for Youth for Christ, says, "The NBEA's strength and weakness has been that it is an association not an organization. This has made it strong and helped facilitate its growth, since a number of organizations with different and distinct missions and organizational goals could come under its umbrella. However, since it could not set the agenda for all of Black evangelicalism, it could only provide a forum for the expression of various views with the objective of mutual fellowship with like-minded evangelical believers."[5]

Dr. Ruth Bentley, who remains one of the pillars of NBEA, says the reason NBEA has not reached its full potential is that in the mid–1970s factions arose, specifically between younger, emerging leaders and the patriarchs. These tended to sabotage and sidetrack the vision.

The NBEA has sought to work in harmony with the White church, encouraging White participation and leadership in its board and program. It has tried to reach out to the community that excluded it and create a context of mutual dialogue and affirmation.

Dr. Bentley and Rev. Knight, early members of NBEA, agree on the following needs for the organization if it is to be influential in the future.

1. The NBEA must return to the vision of its founders as the "place where Black evangelicals could come together for fellowship, networking, and to dialogue on critical issues related to our community."
2. The NBEA must again be supported and affirmed by the Black evangelical wing of the church as a "safe

place where in Christ we can be, regardless of organizational and theological persuasions, as long as the following are affirmed: the person of Christ, salvation by faith alone, and the centrality of the Scriptures."

3. The NBEA must be a bridge of racial reconciliation to the White evangelical church. As such, it can be used by God.

Parachurch Movement

The modern parachurch movement has been an anomaly for many Blacks and Whites. For many in the African American community it has been a nonentity, while for some in the White community it has been the new wine the White evangelical church was seeking. For others it has been an entity that has drained away finances and personnel from the established White evangelical church.

Born out of America's depression, pre–World War II days, the parachurch movement gained momentum and a separate agenda through the Youth for Christ rallies of the forties and fifties and through the crusades of Billy Graham. Beginning with his 1946 Los Angeles crusade, Dr. Graham put to use in a parachurch framework the evangelistic tools and models that had once belonged primarily to the denominations and local churches.

In his book *The Church and the Parachurch Movement*, Jerry White says the parachurch movement arose out of the need on the part of entrepreneurs, driven young leaders of the forties and fifties, who perceived that in evangelism the church was not fully accomplishing its mission.[6] Dawson Trotman, according to his biographer, said, "If the church was not about the business of reaching men for Christ, then God was going to raise up groups outside the church to reach a lost and dying world for him."[7]

Groups such as The Navigators, the Billy Graham Association, Youth for Christ (mother organization of other parachurch groups such as World Vision and Samaritan's Purse), and Campus Crusade for Christ (that now has 18,000 full-time staff members), came into being during this era. Begun by predominately White middle-class males, these groups tended to target White middle-class America.

Mark Senter, youth specialist and professor of Christian education at Trinity Seminary in Deerfield, Illinois, says one of the reasons these groups continue to be primarily monocultural is that those who began the organizations influenced the long-term organizational directions and hindered their ability to translate that vision across cultures.[8]

Institutional racism can be seen in the outworking of the mission of many parachurch organizations. Blinded by quick success, the sponsoring communities seemed unaware of the inherent weaknesses of the organizations in not including minorities in their ministry focus. The perception was that communities of color would not underwrite the ministry. The organizations worked intentionally to maintain and listen to members of their support base. Today some parachurch organizations have fewer Black full-time staff members on board than they did twenty years ago and still do not have African Americans among their senior staff.

Despite these concerns, God has used the conservative evangelical parachurch movement to reach many in the baby boomer and baby buster generations of African Americans. These groups reached many of those who today are the thirty-five- to fifty-year-old evangelical and neo-evangelical leaders in the Black church. The parachurch groups gave these Black leaders their first glimpses of a new perspective of church and the Scriptures. These people have returned to their communities, wanting to see change in the Black church.

Seminaries and Bible Colleges

Conservative theological seminaries and Bible colleges are not far ahead of the parachurch movement in the way of effecting real change for African Americans. Created in the late 1800s and early 1900s as a response to the liberalism of such institutions as Harvard and Yale—formerly the orthodox, conservative training grounds of many ministers in this country—many Bible colleges had a southern root and orientation. Most had little interest in attracting African Americans to their campuses. Many of these schools (not just the schools in the South but across the country) still have less than 1 percent total enrollment of African American students in full-time residential programs, with faculty and senior-level administration represented by an even smaller percentage.

This is not just an institutional problem, and there are no simple answers. Many Blacks within the confines of a historic Black church have not even heard of Christian colleges or institutions of advanced theological training. Even if these Christians have heard of them, they have little interest in them because the institutions do not seem relevant to their community and life. As we saw in chapter 5, many African Americans who believe they have been called into the ministry don't have the same sense of needing seminary training that their counterparts in the White church feel they must pursue.

African Americans who have had exposure to these training systems almost universally come away grateful for the classroom training but frustrated by the cultural and social hurdles they had to endure to receive it.

Curriculum issues are also a concern. College administrators have trouble seeing the value of integrating Black church history into the history curriculum. Seminaries are hesitant to add Black homiletic delivery systems, church management, and styles of leadership to their curriculum.

125

There are other problems that make Christian colleges and evangelical seminaries unattractive to Blacks. These include institutional subculture issues, such as the lack of persons of color in leadership positions, the lack of affirmation for the distinctiveness of African American culture, and the levels of perceived campus community friendliness.

Despite the obstacles within the Black and the White churches, the Black evangelical has emerged, not just as an aberration of the historic Black church, but as new wine, with vitality, energy, and power.

10

Where Do We Go from Here?

The Black Church in the Twenty-first Century and Beyond

One day while driving my son to baseball practice, I began to discuss with him what he will be like when he turns forty. He said to me, "Dad, I guess it doesn't matter to you, because you'll probably be dead anyway." At first I was taken aback, but once I gained my composure I realized he probably was right. The year will be 2022, and not only will his father be different than he is today (if I am still living), but the world around us may not be recognizable. The culture may perceive the Black church (and even, possibly, the church in general) as still on the cutting edge, leading the community, or the church may have continued its current downward spiral to irrelevance.

Being a futurist is a heavy responsibility for one who loves the church. To this point we have looked back to observe and analyze the roots of the Black church in America. But this study would be incomplete if we were not to look forward, examining where the evangelical and neo-evangelical segments of the church should be heading, as compared to where we seem to be heading. I have strong opinions as to where the church—and specifically the Black church—needs to head. Yet after more than two decades of ministry, I cringe at the thought of being a self-appointed prophet.

I will try, however, to make some educated predictions. For the Black evangelical church to continue to grow and make a difference in the community, I believe five strategies need to be pursued.

1. *We need to develop a movement of better-prepared, highly specialized clergy.* With increased availability of higher education for all young people, it is no longer acceptable or effective to allow someone to go into ministry who has experienced a call from God but who has not undergone a focused, formal training that fleshes out the call. As discussed in chapter 5, the traditional pattern of entrance into ministry for the Black pastor was having a subjective experience of being called, being ordained by church leaders, entering into the ministry, and then, in some instances, receiving formal training. Although this was not the course all ministers followed, it was the norm within the Black church.

Today, with a better-informed congregation, the educational and training requirements for pastors are continuing to rise. (This is one of the reasons for the popularity of the relatively recent doctorate of ministries degree that most seminaries now are offering. This degree is typically earned by ministers who already possess a masters of divinity degree. It can usually be earned in four years by attending on a part-time basis, culminating with a dissertation project that is evaluative rather than descriptive or experimental.) This shift in clergy expectations has far-reaching ramifications for the minister and his or her congregation and for the various contexts where this training can take place. Since I am involved in providing undergraduate theological education within an evangelical context, this shift both excites and discourages me. I look at many conservative evangelical seminaries and Bible colleges and question their ability to reach out to and meet the needs of this segment of the population.

2. *Black evangelical churches will move away from the solo full-time pastor (with several unpaid "associate ministers") toward multiple-staff configurations led by one full-time senior pastor.* We are already seeing this phenomenon in many larger congregations. An excellent example of this trend is Dr. Tony Evans's Oak Cliff Bible Fellowship in Dallas. Dr. Evans founded this growing congregation of more than three thousand almost twenty years ago. The church has a wide variety of ministry components led by a large pastoral staff. Another example of this trend is found in the fifteen-hundred–member House of the Lord in Akron, Ohio, where Pastor Joey Johnson leads, with a staff of several full-time pastors.

This model will require a new image of the senior pastor. He or she will be part of a team instead of a Lone Ranger riding off into the sunset to accomplish the mission alone. Still, though part of the team, he or she will be singled out and expected to accomplish more, due to the high priority we as a race put on preaching. I predict that the senior minister will continue to be called on to fulfill the preaching role. This is unlike some White churches (Willow Creek Community Church in Barrington, Illinois, being a trendsetter) where teams of preaching pastors, rather than one main preacher, share the preaching ministry. I do not believe, however, that, given the historical dominance of the Black pastor, we will see team preaching become popular in the Black church.

We will see a retooling of the senior pastor out of the preacher/counselor model to a more visionary leadership model, the forte of whom will be to coordinate and develop his or her staff. As we rethink the pastor's role, there will be a need for more training systems within and outside the church to equip those who serve in such roles.

A significant advantage of larger over smaller churches will be the ability of large churches to underwrite financially the increased cost of multiple ministry staff and the resulting ministry opportunities. In these congregations the pastors will reap benefits from the shared workload and will see their churches grow because of their ability to focus on a particular area of ministry.

3. We will see a continued emphasis on ministry to community from a holistic perspective. Ministry from a holistic perspective means seeing the gospel worked out in the life of an individual, not only spiritually but emotionally and physically. Dr. John Perkins is the "father" of holistic ministry in the United States. His philosophy is capsulized in his "three Rs of Christian community development." He believes ministry is best done by those who are willing to *relocate* into the target community as participants rather than outsiders. He believes that *reconciliation* is the heartbeat of the gospel and is essential to effective ministry. And he believes in the long-lasting benefits of *redistribution* of resources. Only as redistribution of wealth takes place and the poor become more self-sufficient will change occur. America's problem is not a race problem, ultimately, but an economic one.

This understanding of the need for holistic ministry has always been a strong suit of the Black church. In its context, the Black church could not afford to dichotomize the gospel, making it strictly spiritual. It's only been within the last fifteen years, though, that the evangelical segment of the Black church has come to embrace and apply this truth to its context. In my opinion, this trend needs to increase.

4. *We will need to target ministries to dysfunctional and single-parent families.* More than half of the families in the Black community (this is even higher in some inner-core communities) are fatherless. Crack cocaine babies flood the hospitals; AIDS is rampant in the Black community (in proportion higher than in the majority community); abortion and sexual and physical abuse are prevalent; an economic disparity continues to characterize these communities.

In the last two decades northern inner-city communities have come to view the Black church—at one time the most vocal and strategic institution in the Black community—as irrelevant. The church must regain the confidence of her constituency by ministering to the felt needs of families and individuals. People who don't know Jesus can see him only through his people, reaching out to them in compassion and with practical help.

5. *We will see the Black church place a greater emphasis on expository preaching.* Expository preaching focuses on explanation of Scripture and expounding on a text through the interpretation of the author's original intent. It allows the Scripture text to drive the message, rather than the messenger or the context driving it. We will need to see this method of preaching carried out more carefully within the cultural construct of the Black church.

One of the main strengths of the Black church has been its emotional fervor and the comfort God's people have taken from the preaching of his Word. The problem has been, however, in the area of relevancy. Preaching within today's and tomorrow's Black church must focus on the Scripture's sufficiency to meet deeper spiritual needs that move beyond emotional response. This is an even greater need today as we move into the postmodern era of relative truth. Absolutes will continue to be disdained. We'll need to hear clear, concise teaching of Scripture that alone is profitable to equip us for every good deed.

A secondary challenge is reaching an intellectually more advanced generation (the huge number of baby boomers as well as baby busters). The Black church is seeing among its adult ranks the first generation of Blacks who have in large numbers attended institutions of higher learning. These parishioners demand messages that are more structured in delivery and more content based. People want not only to hear good music, but to hear a message from God through his Word.

This greater emphasis on expository preaching will have great impact on the more traditional aspects of the institutional Black church. Those movements that embrace the African American tradition and then go beyond it through expository preaching of God's truth will attract a younger membership who are more used to this method of information delivery.

I believe the Black church in the twenty-first century will continue to hold a strong place of allegiance in the hearts and minds of Black people. To move ahead in this rapidly changing culture, though, its leaders will have to think new thoughts, do new things, and create new paradigms of worship and expressions of faith. Jesus said almost two thousand years ago that he was going to build his church, and nothing—not even the gates of hell—would prevail against it. As we look to the future, let us be ever mindful that it is not a Black church or a White church we are talking about, but his church.

—11—

Evangelical Ministries in the African American Community

The purpose of this chapter is to familiarize the reader with some present-day ministries in the African American community. Many of these organizations are distinct, not only because of the site of their ministry, but because they are led by African Americans.

Ralph Ellison's classic novel *The Invisible Man* was revolutionary for its time as it dealt with the isolation and rejection of the African American in society. The term "the invisible man" may also reflect perceptions of where the evangelical witness is in the Black community. But just as Ellison's hero was not really invisible, neither is the evangelical church. The Black evangelical church is not only alive, it has the potential to exert its greatest influence as the new millennium approaches. In this chapter we will look at contemporary models of evangelical ministry that have targeted the African American community. This chapter can be used as a networking tool that can bring more Christians in touch with God's work in the African American community.

This list of ministries is far from exhaustive. I do not intend to imply that these are the only viable evangelical ministries within the Black community. But they are representative of what is there and they should give us hope in knowing that the Black community has not been forgotten by the evangelical church.

Educational Institutions

Carver Bible Institute and College, Atlanta, Georgia

Carver Bible Institute and College was founded in the fall of 1943. It is one of the oldest, continuously operating Bible institutes that focuses on training men and women for Christian leadership within the Black community. Founded by Talmage and Grace Payne, veteran missionaries to China, it began in a storefront and has grown into a campus of several buildings and has a current enrollment of approximately 110 students. During the 1963–64 school year Dr. and Mrs. Payne retired, and the school's dean, Dr. William D. Hungerpillar, became president.

Three blocks from downtown Atlanta, the campus is compact and adjacent to residential areas. In 1968 the present administration building was constructed, housing a dining room, offices, and classrooms. A library, a gymnasium, and married student housing have become part of the expanding campus.

The Institute's statement of purpose says: "Carver Bible Institute and College is a professional school of higher education which specializes in training adults for Christian service."[1] Every student has a Bible major; the Word of God is at the core of the curriculum. All liberal arts courses are taught from the viewpoint of Scripture.

Carver offers: a B.A. degree in Bible, a B.A. in biblical studies, a Bachelor of Theology degree (for those who hold a bachelor's degree from another institution), an Associate of Arts degree, and a diploma in Bible. Minors in missions and pastoral studies are also available.[2]

Baptist Bible College of Indianapolis, Indianapolis, Indiana

Baptist Bible College of Indianapolis was born in 1980 out of the vision of James Wells, pastor of the Zion Hope Baptist Church. Under his leadership and dynamic expository preaching, Zion Hope grew from thirty-five to five hundred members. Outgrowing its building, it purchased the facilities of the Devington Baptist Church on the city's northeast side. At this location the school was born, with fifty students in its inaugural year. Dr. Wells remained president until his death in September 1987.

From its inception, the school focused on training African American Christian leaders and preachers to evangelize metropolitan areas of America.[3] Early in 1980 Dr. Wells invited Ken Davis, missionary pastor of the largely African American Trinity Baptist Church in Indianapolis and Clint Kaufield, an experienced pastor, to work with him in organizing the school. Both of these men helped raise funds for the school.

Baptist Bible College has grown, not only under Dr. Wells's direction, but currently under the direction of Dr. Charles Ware, who became the school's second president in 1991. In 1988 the school relocated to a larger facility but by 1996 had outgrown that building and has recently moved again.

The college boasts a faculty of seventeen and draws students from Indiana, several other states, and foreign countries. It offers three academic programs:

- A four-year Bachelor of Religious Education degree to prepare men and women for full-time vocational ministry. Students choose a concentration in pastoral studies, urban/ethnic ministries, international missions, local church education, or elementary education.
- A two-year Associate of Religious Education degree for lay leaders.
- A one-year certificate in biblical studies for those coming from or going to secular colleges.

At this writing, Baptist Bible College is seeking full accreditation with the Accrediting Association of Bible Colleges.[4]

Southern Bible Institute, Dallas, Texas

Southern Bible Institute, an interdenominational institution, trains men and women of any color in the truth of Scripture, realizing the great need of all people is an understanding of the Word of God.[5] The school trains vocational and avocational pastors, missionaries, and teachers and accepts students who may not have received highly academic training.

The school began in 1927 with three students meeting in the home of Edmund H. Ironside, then a student at Dallas Seminary. Founded under the name Dallas Colored Bible Institute, the Institute's board was chaired by Dr. H. A. Ironside with Dr. Edmund H. Ironside as its first president. He served until his death in 1941.

On June 1, 1945, Dr. Henderson S. Fox became president. That summer the school purchased three lots at 1415 Fleetwood Street that soon made up the campus. In 1976 the school moved to 830 South Buckner, tripling the size of the campus. Dr. Fox retired in June 1971. Rev. Gordon Mumford became president in July 1974.

While the school offers no degrees, it grants a diploma to those who complete the entire forty-eight hours of Bible curriculum.[6]

Publishing Companies

Black Light Fellowship, Chicago, Illinois

Founded in 1976 by Rev. and Mrs. Walter McCray, Black Light Fellowship's purpose is to "disciple Black folk into Christ-centered Black nationhood," according to Rev. McCray. The company offers holistic curriculum materials for Christian Black education.

"Black Light Fellowship is business/ministry. Our purpose is to make money and to do ministry through the money we make. We are a multifaceted media company, specializing currently in publishing, a bookstore, a conference center, mission work in Africa, and other entrepreneurial ventures," Rev. McCray says.[7]

Urban Ministries Inc., Calumet City, Illinois

Melvin Banks founded Urban Ministries Inc. (UMI) in 1970. It is the fulfillment of his boyhood dream. Now located at 1551 Regency Court in Calumet City, UMI began in the basement of Dr. Banks's home. While working at the Scripture Press Company, he realized the need for resources appropriate for urban Black Christians. The first publications, introduced in January 1971, were *Inteen* and *Inteen Teacher*. Urban Ministries has grown to employ seventy-two full- and part-time employees and is the nation's leading Black evangelical publisher of Sunday school and vacation Bible school curricula.

The company's products are available through denominational publishing houses, bookstores across the country, and directly through a sales force of telemarketing and field sales personnel.[8]

137

A highlight of the ministry is the company's annual Christian education/Sunday school convention held each October in Chicago.[9]

Renaissance Productions, Inc., Woodbury, New Jersey

Renaissance Productions, Inc. was founded by Dr. Tony Evans (senior pastor of Oak Cliff Bible Fellowship and president of the Urban Alternative in Dallas) and Roland G. Hardy Jr. (Roland G. Hardy & Associates, Woodbury, New Jersey) in June 1988. The company provides religious and theological materials to people of color. "Renaissance designs resources that model a holistic philosophy of ministry in economic development and empowerment in urban and African American communities."[10]

In 1986 Mr. Hardy became executive vice president of the Urban Alternative. From 1985 to 1988 as Dr. Evans and Mr. Hardy traveled on behalf of the Urban Alternative, it became evident that people in the urban African American community were struggling with Christianity because of the growing perception that it is a White man's religion. Hardy and Evans agreed resources had to be developed to address this need. By 1992 the company had generated $275,000 in gross sales and continues to grow in market share.

Renaissance utilizes an integrated approach to distributing its resources:

- Bookstores. "Although the vast majority of our target audience does not purchase Christian resources from bookstores, there is a growing number of bookstores that service our community."[11]
- Networking. According to the Direct Selling Association (DSA), direct selling accounted for 14.1 bil-

lion dollars in sales in 1992, up 45 percent from 1988.[12]

- Church Direct. Churches purchase resources directly from Renaissance at a discounted price.
- Direct Mail. Renaissance uses its customer list of ten thousand for its direct mailings.[13]

Parachurch/Mission Organizations

Legacy Ministries, Atlanta, Georgia

Legacy, a ministry of Campus Crusade for Christ, helps rebuild and restore the spiritual heritage of urban America by creating a positive environment for evangelism and discipleship. Directed by speaker and author Dr. Crawford Loritts Jr., Legacy has several ministries that target the urban family, in efforts to return it to wholeness:

- Mentoring. Programs in urban schools bring together children and Christian adults for private tutoring, motivation, and support.
- Urban family conferences. Two-day seminars communicate God's plan for a strong family.
- Ministry to single parents. Seventy percent of African American families will be headed by a female by 2000. The need for individual discipleship and resources for parenting, financial management, and other areas of growth is overwhelming.
- Bible studies for couples. These small-group Bible studies help couples build strong, lasting marriages.
- Women's ministry. This ministry's focus is evangelism and discipleship of urban business and professional women.[14]

Institute of Black Family Development, Detroit, Michigan

The Institute of Black Family Development began in January 1987 as a response to Bill Moyer's March 1986 documentary "The Vanishing Black Family: A Crisis in America."[15]

The Institute provides training, consulting, and family resources to improve the quality of life for children and families through the church. The Institute has been involved in or helped in the formation of:

- The pastors development ministry. In cooperation with Mendenhall Ministries this service trains 250 pastors and wives every year.
- Michigan Leadership Fund. High schoolers are trained to become leaders.
- National Summit on Black Church Development. This biannual conference began in 1986 and has grown to a by-invitation-only summit of more than 150 key ministry leaders from across the nation.
- Family Life University (previously the National Conference on the Family). Training, networking, and resources are provided in the area of family ministry.
- Publication. Several books related to the family have been published with Moody Press and Zondervan Publishing House.

The objectives of the Institute of Black Family Development are:

1. To assist those involved in the church to meet the needs of families and to carry out ministry to other families in the community.
2. To establish in the existing church a Christian perspective and response to the needs of families.

3. To develop a national data bank to network the church and enrich existing ministries to families.[16]

Chicago Urban Reconciliation Enterprise (CURE), Chicago, Illinois

The Chicago Urban Reconciliation Enterprise is a collaboration of racially diverse urban Christians with the goal of helping urban churches impact youth. The organization was founded in June of 1986 by Rev. Russell Knight, who is still the president, and a group of urban youth workers (both Black and White) whose burden for urban youth had become an all-consuming passion.

CURE provides quality training to urban youth workers. Their ministries include consulting, leadership training, an annual youth convention, facilitation and reconciliation services, and production of helpful, creative, and inexpensive material for today's urban youth worker.

The CURE cross-cultural team discovered that traditional approaches to urban youth work were not getting the job done, so they committed themselves to creating ministry models that worked and to training volunteers from local churches.[17] CURE training ranges from one-day seminars to ongoing consulting.

As this team has trained workers across America, they have produced simple models that can be duplicated in all local settings. These are ministries that CURE workers have successfully used. For example, Rev. Knight and his wife have developed innovative programs that they run out of their home:

- An after-school homework club and collectors club for youth from ages 5–18
- A neighborhood club with wholesome recreation as a gang alternative

- An international hospitality house with guests from around the world or from down the block
- A small-group ministry to youth or men called "Take Five"
- An emergency assistance fund for short-term community needs[18]

Urban Evangelical Mission (formerly Black Evangelistic Enterprises), Dallas, Texas

Urban Evangelical Mission was founded in 1973 by Dr. Ruben Conner. Dr. Conner began his church-planting ministry in 1960 when he and his wife Geneva founded the Second Avenue Mission, renamed Community Bible Church, at 1227 Hendricks Street. In 1973 Black Evangelistic Enterprises was born out of a vision to see more evangelical Bible churches planted in Black, urban areas across the country. In 1994 the name was changed to Urban Evangelical Mission.

This ministry has helped establish evangelical churches in nineteen states as far east as West Palm Beach, Florida, and as far west as Phoenix, under the leadership of Dr. Conner.

Urban Evangelical Mission accomplishes its mission of evangelizing and discipling African Americans by:

- Planting evangelical churches in major urban centers that will reproduce themselves
- Evangelizing urban communities through gospel presentations, literature, and other strategies
- Developing urban church planters through regional seminars, internships, evaluations, and assessments
- Equipping growing churches to reach the urban population through holistic ministry[19]

142

Economic and Community Development Agencies

Lawndale Community Church, Chicago, Illinois

The motto "We develop people, not programs" accurately communicates the thrust of the Lawndale Community Church. In 1975 Wayne Gordon, a White former high school football coach and Carey Casey, a Black former football star and national staff worker for the Fellowship of Christian Athletes, formed a biracial partnership and founded the ministry. Until recently Rev. Casey pastored the growing, inner-city church. Wayne Gordon is the church's outreach pastor and the executive director of Lawndale Community Ministries (the church's multimillion-dollar community outreach component).

Lawndale Community Church touches the lives of thousands of residents of the economically depressed South Lawndale neighborhood through its creative programs. Based on the racial reconciliation, relocation, and redistribution model Dr. John Perkins established in Mendenhall, Mississippi, Lawndale has developed a housing development corporation, the largest outpatient medical clinic on the South Side, innovative business and partnership ventures that are revitalizing the community, educational computer and scholarship programs, and a myriad of youth- and family-centered holistic ministries that are supported by a full-time staff of 135.[20]

Voice of Calvary/Jackson and Mendenhall Ministries, Mendenhall, Mississippi

John Perkins and his wife Vera Mae, burdened for their native Mississippi, began ministering a holistic gospel that met the physical, spiritual, and emotional needs of the people. Two ministries were born from their efforts: Mendenhall Ministries and Voice of Calvary in Jackson. They are models of economic and community development for the

143

evangelical community. Raised in racist, violent Mississippi, Dr. Perkins moved to California in the 1950s to escape the segregation and oppression of the Deep South. He had no intention of returning to Mississippi, but God had a different plan. Dr. Perkins came to know Christ through the ministry of Child Evangelism Fellowship. Godly White Christians from CEF discipled and befriended John Perkins, demonstrating that they loved him for who he was in Christ.

Dr. Perkins felt God calling him back to Mendenhall to minister to his people, despite the racial hatred and strife that still existed there. He soon began to formulate the foundational philosophical and theological undergirding that would support not only his ministry in Mississippi, but other ministries around the country: his holistic ministry philosophy of reconciliation, redistribution, and relocation. These three Rs have revolutionized ministry to the poor in rural and urban areas.

A co-op store, clothing distribution site, housing ministry, community economic development programs, health care clinics, and youth ministries operate at the two Mississippi sites.[21]

Christian Community Development Association (CCDA), Chicago, Illinois

In 1989 Dr. John Perkins called a group of Christian leaders from across America to Chicago. These individuals were bonded by their commitment to expressing Christ's love to America's poor communities at the grass-roots level and together they formed an association—the Christian Community Development Association. CCDA has grown from thirty-seven founding members to three thousand individuals and three hundred churches, with ministries in thirty-five states and more than one hundred cities.

Led by John Perkins as chairman and Wayne Gordon as president, CCDA is grounded in Dr. Perkins's three Rs philosophy: relocation (the importance of living among the people we minister to), reconciliation (loving our neighbor as a reflection of the reality of God), and redistribution (sharing our faith by being willing to reallocate resources to those less fortunate).

CCDA is a fellowship of like-minded Christian churches, ministries, families, and individuals who learn from each other. It provides member organizations with ministry support in training, technical assistance in community and economic development, job referral service, program evaluation, and networking.[22]

Circle Urban Ministries, Chicago, Illinois

Circle Urban Ministries began in 1974 with a simple understanding of the need to serve the poor. Several White families from Circle Church (pastored by a Black man, Clarence Hillard, and a White man, David Mains) felt God's call to move into the predominately Black, impoverished community of Austin. Their church's desire to reach out in love to those around them fueled their passion. One of these initial families was Glen and Lonnie Kehrein. Glen would eventually become executive director of this fledgling ministry and remains in that position. The ministry has evolved into a multimillion-dollar, multiracial organization that ministers holistically to its community in the name of Christ.

Breaking the cycle of poverty required more than theology. It required that the gospel be lived out in the community. This has been the guiding focus of this ministry.

Circle offers ten programs in the Austin community:

1. Chaplaincy. Circle's chaplaincy ministry keeps its door open to those who are hurting and broken.

145

2. Emergency care. Hundreds of families have received food, clothing, and shelter during crisis times.

3. Economic development. Many Austin residents have found employment through the businesses Circle has established, including its manufacturing business.

4. Adult education. Adults are learning to read, acquire academic skills, and earn their GED diplomas.

5. Youth. Through Inside Circle, young people have found a haven, love, and acceptance from caring adults.

6. Education. Quality education is scarce in the inner city. Circle is attempting to address this need by developing elementary and secondary schools.

7. Legal aid. The urban community needs advocates, operating out of a Christian worldview, who can represent those who are underrepresented in society.

8. Health care. Families receive affordable health care through Circle's outpatient clinic.

9. Housing. Circle has restored hundreds of apartment units and several homes in the community.

10. Tutoring. Children who need extra help receive one-on-one tutoring.

Circle's vision was further enhanced when in 1983 Raleigh Washington, a recent graduate of Trinity Evangelical Seminary and a former career military officer, moved into the Austin community to begin the Rock of Our Salvation Evangelical Free Church. This four-hundred–member interracial church (70 percent Black and 30 percent White) has partnered with Circle Urban Ministries to live out the love of Christ in this community.[23]

Westside Holistic Family Services, Chicago, Illinois

"Westside Holistic Family services is a Christian, community-based, minority agency that ministers to individuals and families through a holistic approach that brings about physical, emotional, psychological, educational, and spiritual well-being."[24] The agency targets the Austin and West Garfield Park communities.

The ministry was founded in 1979 by Lloyd and Milicent Lindo. Lloyd is senior pastor of Keystone Baptist Church on the west side of Chicago and Milicent is the executive director of Westside Holistic Family Services.

The organization encompasses various ministries, such as individual and group counseling, health care, literacy programs, vocational training programs, and many others.[25]

Media: TV and Radio Ministries

The Alternative, Dallas, Texas

The Alternative is the radio ministry of Dr. Tony Evans, Senior Pastor of Oak Cliff Bible Fellowship. Dr. Evans is the first evangelical African American to launch a national, daily, thirty-minute Bible teaching program. The program is one part of the rapidly growing ministry to the urban community led by Dr. Evans known as the Urban Alternative. More than 250 radio stations across the country air *The Alternative*, taught by Dr. Evans. Known for its expositional nature and African American style, *The Alternative* attracts Black and White listeners.[26]

Glenn Plummer and Associates, Detroit, Michigan

Glenn Plummer is a pioneer among evangelical African American broadcasters. He is the president and founder of Christian TV Network, based in Southfield, Michigan. This production company has provided wholesome, Christ-

147

centered family entertainment via broadcast and cable TV since 1982. Plummer and his organization have a passion to see the urban church equipped to become more effective.

Christian TV Network owns two stations (in the Detroit and New Orleans markets) and produces *Blessing*, a half-hour, weekly program, and a daily talk show called *LTN Live*. It is the only TV production company in the United States that is owned and operated by African American evangelicals.[27]

The Strategic Role
of the Black Church

Very few people in America, whether Black or White, would disagree that the Black church has been the preeminent institution in the history of the Black experience in America. Whether it be as the cradle of the Underground Railroad movement during slavery or the catalyst for the civil rights movement of the 1950s and 60s, the Black church has been and continues to be a primary influence in the Black community. For this reason I am convinced that any plan to revitalize our cities and empower Black people will never be effective without some type of strategic impact of the Black church, especially as it relates to the moral and spiritual development of our people.

If the church plays such a strategic role in the Black community, the question then must be asked, Why have our communities continued to deteriorate? With such a complex and multifaceted issue, there is obviously no way that this paper or any other could do full justice to this question. However, I believe a key part of the problem is that although the Black church has exerted strong political and social leadership, it has been lacking spiritual leadership; those who have received the type of training that will enable them to rightly divide the Word of God. This is true particularly over the last fifty years of our experience in this country. It is my intent in this short paper to address, in an overview fashion, the issue of the need for better trained pastoral leadership, focusing on the critical need in the Black church for the development of godly, well-trained, visionary leadership. These leaders must not only see the value of training within a formal educational context, but must also be empowered by the evangelical community to become the much needed catalyst for proactive and long-term change in our communities through the effective ministry of the local church.

In order to address this issue, I have decided to focus on the three fundamental issues related to fulfilling the need for advanced theological and biblical training within the Black church. They are as follows:

1. A historical perspective as to why effective development of spiritual leadership has failed to occur within the evangelical conservative wing of the church
2. An understanding of the nature of the call to ministry for most African American leaders and how this process differs from our Anglo brothers and sisters
3. A look at institutional racism within conservative theological settings, and a suggestion as to how conservative, evangelical seminaries, Bible colleges, and Christian liberal arts colleges can become more proactive in their ability to not only reach, but also to embrace, empower, and equip those who have been called to minister within an African American context

Historical Perspective on the Lack of Formal Advanced Theological Training for African Americans within Conservative Evangelical Settings

Historically, African Americans are some of the most bibliocentric people within the framework of the American society. One of the primary reasons that Blacks were able to endure the two-hundred-year horror of slavery was Scripture, and specifically its adaptation to song in the form of the Negro spiritual. During this time the Black preacher was one of the few people who could read. Even after slavery the Black preacher was one of the most educated people in the community, especially during the Reconstruction period on into the twentieth century. Spiritual values were the driving force behind most African Americans' views of the world.

This began to change for many as Blacks moved from the South in the late 1800s and early 1900s into urban areas, during what is known as the Great Migration period. Literally thousands of Blacks left the rural South to find their fortune in northern industrialized cities. The North was seen as the Black man's promised land, yet many arrived in this unfamiliar environment only to find even worse conditions than what they had left in the South. The Black church, the only stable institution under Black leadership, became even more important as not only a cultural link to the South but also as the catalyst by which Blacks might gain some sense of political, social, and economic empowerment in a racist society. The Black church, thus, was seen not so much as the guardian of spiritual and biblical values, but as the one place through which Blacks could develop and have some sense of economic and political ownership. The Black preacher, therefore, had to increasingly develop the skills of a community, political, and economic leader. The preacher's role as spiritual undershepherd diminished, along with the recognition of the need for more advanced biblical training.

Almost simultaneously was the beginning of what is called the Great Fundamentalist controversy. Up to the mid-1800s, schools such as Yale, Harvard, and Princeton had been the primary centers of advanced theological training of ministers in this country. As these schools began to turn liberal in their theology, they were replaced by theological institutions that believed in Bible inerrancy and the orthodox views of the church. Even though these institutions were more conservative and fundamental in their theology, and thus from my perspective better equipped to prepare people for ministry, they were incorrect sociologically, for they were institutionally insensitive in not allowing African Americans to be a part of their institutions, even up to recent times. They had the right words, but the wrong behavior. Especially within the evangelical persuasion, this broadened the gap between the Black and the White church. It also hindered those within the Black community from receiving the necessary training needed to be more effective in their ministry.

The role of the Black church, as the only viable vehicle to meet the overwhelming needs of the Black community within a racist society, combined with the exclusionary and racist practices of the more conservative, evangelical seminaries, served to create a training gap that to this day has not been overcome. This was worsened as the second historical cause became more evident, the creation of a backlash within the Black community towards these institutions of higher education, reinforcing the perception that Blacks would be selling out on their race to even consider going to such schools.

The Call to Ministry within the African American Context

The second fundamental issue to be addressed in looking at the critical need for advanced training within the

African American church is the whole issue of the call to ministry as it relates to how this differs from the majority community. For example, most of us as African American leaders first received the call to ministry, then went into ministry, got ordained, and *then*, and only in some situations, received some type of formal education. On the other hand, those in the majority community tend to receive the call to ministry, pursue advanced training, get ordained, and then go out in to ministry. This fundamental difference in the experience of Black versus White leaders has caused the following repercussions:

1. Many Black leaders, if they do pursue some type of formal training, pursue it later in life.
2. Due to the additional responsibilities they have, such as family and jobs (many pastors are bivocational and must have employment outside of their pastorate), many Black leaders are not able to take advantage of educational opportunities that might be present.
3. Ministry responsibilities might be a hindrance to pursuing advanced training since these pastors are typically further along in their ministry than their White counterparts.
4. The likelihood of seeing the need for more training is diminished. For example, it is difficult for a man with a church of five hundred to see the need to go to seminary when most of the Blacks with that training whom he has met have either a very limited experience base or have ministries that would never measure up to his in terms of numbers.

Institutional Racism within Conservative Theological Settings

The third fundamental issue in looking at some of the systemic barriers to advanced biblical training within the

Black church is the need to recognize the reality of institutional racism within conservative evangelical settings and develop steps that will enable training institutions to embrace, empower, and equip those who are called to minister within the African American community. Institutional racism, from my perspective, is the exclusion of various groups of individuals, usually very subtly, from equal access to the main power structures of an organization and thus exclusion from equal opportunity to share in these power structures, simply on the basis of race. In discussing the reality of institutional racism within the context of conservative theological settings, three very important concerns come to the forefront:

1. The inconsistency between a theology that says we are one in Christ and a practice, both in history as well as currently, that has at best limited the participation of Blacks within these institutions
2. The need to systematically address the issue of equal access and opportunities for African Americans versus responding in a piecemeal or reactive mode
3. A suggested starting point in which some of these issues could be addressed

Examining the Inconsistency of a Right Theology but Wrong Sociology

In taking a survey of some of the leading conservative institutions of higher education, five major factors emerged.

1. The inability of the Anglo/majority culture to understand the impact of institutional climate and culture on the African American student, especially within the context of racist America
2. The inability of the dominant culture to understand the importance of infrastructure in terms of building

"bridges" for those whose experience is different than the majority culture

3. The inability of the dominant culture to separate what is cultural, and therefore negotiable, with what is biblical, and therefore must be held dear no matter what

4. The inability of the dominant culture to understand the need for repentance of the sin of slavery and its impact on the Christian community even today

5. The inability of the dominant culture, especially within institutions of higher education, to understand the necessity of instituting a policy of competency-based learning equivalents if one is to reach the majority of African American church leaders

Let's look at each one of these.

Impact of Institutional Climate and Culture

The dominant culture is unable to understand the impact of institutional climate and culture on those who seek to be assimilated from outside the particular cultural norm that is exposed.

Institutional culture is inevitably expressed in what an organization values and does. These are rooted in the organization's history, saga, and development, that are reflected within a certain organizational climate. Within Christian institutions, which have the Bible as their focus of living and thinking, the dominant influence would ideally be the fact that they are Christian. Unfortunately, all too often it is not the Bible that drives an institutional climate but rather the culture of the dominant, majority group. In the instance of evangelical institutions of higher education, this problem reinforces the need to continually work on creating a "friendly" instead of "hostile" environment for those African Americans who must somehow figure out how to assimilate into a culture that is totally foreign to them. What this tells the student is that true success is measured by how close they can talk, think, and look like the dominant culture. This creates a hostile environment from the point of view that it enforces a certain cultural frame of reference that only accepts the values and norms of one culture as correct.

Building Bridges

The second reason that we see inconsistency within evangelical institutions of higher education is the inability and, in some cases unwillingness to understand the need to provide the necessary "bridges" (academic support systems) that enable an African American student to be successful in a "hostile" environment. This is of critical importance if one whose experience is different would still be able to achieve access and opportunity.

The 1960s and early '70s saw the upswing of affirmative action and equal access programs not only in the business community but also in the area of higher education. Both secular and Christian institutions of training began to admit the need to be more inclusive of minorities in general, and Blacks specifically, within their structures. "Bridges" from the Black community to the Anglo-dominated higher education system included programs such as equal opportunity, summer tutorial programs like Upward Bound for high school students interested in attending college, and special financial aid and other support services. The Christian community was slower in implementing some of these very important infrastructure bridges.

The '80s saw a retrenchment from many of the services afforded African American students in the late '60s and early '70s. This occurred as society shifted to a more conservative ideology and thus began to withdraw some of the programs and services that had been won under the politically more liberal Democratic Party during the height of the civil rights

156

era in the '60s. This retrenchment was even greater within evangelical institutions of learning, especially due to the fact that most of these Christian schools did not have the enormous resources that public, governmental-funded institutions of higher education had. It is crucial that evangelical seminaries, Bible colleges, and Christian schools today seek to understand and develop the necessary "Bridges" or infrastructure by which African Americans can be successful. This is critical because of the fact that many African Americans have not received the foundational grammatical, literary, and other educational skills to compete on this level.

Separating the Cultural from the Biblical

The third reason why the dichotomy exists between the words and the actions of conservative evangelical seminaries, Bible colleges, and Christian liberal arts colleges in the area of equal access and opportunity is the inability of the dominant culture to separate what is biblical from what is simply cultural. Music preference is a classic example of acceptable cultural distinctions that need to be affirmed, not looked down upon. In reality, this is only one example that has been forged through the crucible of the dominant culture's experience. This tendency to fail to distinguish what is biblical from what is merely cultural, occurs not only in such areas as music, but in our theological presuppositions as well, particularly since theology, man's attempt to define God, is developed through the grid of one's culture, for example, the issue of the role of the church politically. Most people in the Black community see no inconsistency between the pastor and his political involvement. What is cultural must be distinguished from that which is biblical.

Repentance of the Sin of Slavery

The fourth reason why the inconsistency exists between the words and actions of evangelical training institutions,

157

which thus continues to reinforce institutional racism as a system, is the inability of the dominant culture to see their need to repent from the sin of slavery and understand its impact not only on Black culture but American culture in general. Many wonder how slavery is relevant to them, especially as they themselves did not actually enslave anyone. Beyond this, how could this relate to institutional racism within Christian higher education structures? Even though they were not alive during slavery and therefore could not have helped perpetuate this two-hundred-year atrocity, members of today's dominant society have continued to reap the benefits, economically and socially, of a system of oppression, a system that literally destroyed millions of Blacks and laid the foundation for the gross economic, social, and political disparity between Blacks and Whites. Second Chronicles 7:14 says, "If my people, who are called by my name, will humble themselves and pray and seek my face and turn from their wicked ways, then will I hear from heaven and will forgive their sin and will heal their land." This is especially true for the evangelical conservative wing of the church, which has for the most part stood on the sidelines of racial oppression and inequality. It has even allowed the church to perpetuate a "separate but equal" mentality within its confines, seen within the structures of Christian higher education.

Competency-based Learning Equivalents

The last issue related to the inconsistency of profession and practice of evangelical higher education structures is the unwillingness to validate with academic credit an experiential, life-related, competency-based model of learning experiences. Chicago State University, located in Chicago, has an outstanding program known as the Board of Governors Program, which recognizes the fact that:

1. The traditional 18–24-year-old student population is shrinking. For an institution to be viable, it must go after the adult learner.

2. Adults have acquired a great deal of skill and concept learning through nonformal life situations. As it relates to training for ministry, 95 percent of all those involved as pastors and ministers in the Black church will never go to seminary. Yet these individuals have a great deal of skill and concept development, which should be validated and augmented. The result of this type of accreditation would create greater access for many who are not willing or able to invest in three to four years of full-time theological training.

Institutional Racism: A Systems Approach

In looking at institutional racism, then, the first critical issue that must be addressed is the need to recognize the reality of institutional racism within the conservative evangelical sector of the church and the importance of beginning to deal with the discrepancy between what is professed and what is practiced. Second, we must begin to systematically analyze what the roots of the issue are, as attempted in this monograph. We cannot look at these issues in a piecemeal, reactionary mode, such as during times of crises (often the pattern by Christian institutions of higher education). We need to build a systems model within institutions that continually deals with the complex issues surrounding this problem.

Long-term change can be ensured only through a systematic approach. This can be seen in the changes that occurred during the '60s. During this time, African Americans, who to this point had been on the periphery of society, were able to face greater possibility of inclusion into the mainstream of American life. However, the forces that made this possible, such as the civil rights movement and the enactment of certain federal statutes, were created out of a more reactive than proactive mode. In other words, changes were instituted by those on the outside (Martin Luther King Jr. and the civil rights movement) and was never the settled agenda for the power brokers of this country. For this very reason, the great progress made through legislative and social was rather short-term and superficial.

This same phenomenon occurred within the evangelical, conservative wing of the church, within both denominations and schools of higher learning. In the late '60s and early '70s, conservative theological seminaries and Bible colleges were bombarded by external forces to become more diverse, not only in terms of student enrollment but also in terms of curriculum, faculty diversification, and so on. Blacks specifically were targeted to become part of these institutions. A few years after the popularity of the civil rights movement had subsided and the conservative philosophies of Richard Nixon and others refocused the direction of our country away from social activism to economic individualism, Black students suddenly found themselves on the outside again. What had been implemented, even though good, could not be sustained because it had been created more as a reaction to outside forces than as an institutional commitment to the direction of much needed diversity.

What differentiates the reactive versus the systemic approach? The illustration comes to mind of a young boy who broke his arm in two places while playing football. He needed both an immediate and long-term cure, but was told by the trainer that all he needed was a Band-Aid and some pain medicine, even though his problem was more serious. Historically, reactive approaches within Christian higher education tend to put Band-Aids on deep and long-term problems. This gives only an illusion of health with no long-term cure. Systematic solutions, on the other hand, see the problem from a systems point of view. They recognize that unless a problem is dealt with systematically, it will only provide short-term fixes to deep and long-term problems. They also recognize that because these problems are interconnected, they will continue to cause more problems unless dealt with at their interconnected roots.

Institutional Racism: Developing a Strategy

Finally, the issue of institutional racism must be looked at in terms of developing, at least in a simplified form, an action plan to deal with this issue, based on a response to the five critical factors identified earlier in this paper.

Response to factor 1. Develop a commitment to ongoing, cross-cultural and multiracial sensitivity training for all staff, administrators, and faculty.

Response to factor 2. Identify at minimum five training institutions of comparable size and study what types of bridges have been implemented and the effect of each.

Response to factor 3. Set up a curriculum revision task force. The specific agenda of this committee would be to analyze the curriculum from the perspective of what is simply cultural and not scriptural.

Response to factor 4. Implement a Day of Prayer and Fasting as it relates to the issue of the sin of slavery and its effect on the Christian community today.

Response to factor 5. Research the possibility of developing competency-based learning structures, which would be used to empower minorities with significant experience to receive academic credit for their work. A portfolio or some type of measuring instrument would be required.

Embracing, Empowering, and Equipping: A Call to the Evangelical Church

The Black church continues to play a major role of strategic importance within the Black community. The

161

need for increased development of spiritual leadership is great, yet many factors have blocked advanced theological training for African Americans in evangelical circles. The tragedy of a right theology but wrong sociology cannot be understated. The Christ who died to break down the barriers is the Christ in whom we are one. Evangelical institutions of higher learning must commit to proactively addressing the issues surrounding theological education for African American leaders, and together let us work toward embracing, empowering, and equipping those called to minister within the African American community.

Notes

Chapter 1: *Separate and Unequal*

1. Anthony T. Evans, *Are Blacks Spiritually Inferior to Whites?: The Dispelling of an American Myth* (Wenonah, N.J.: Renaissance Productions, 1992), 71.

2. August Meier and Elliott Rudwick, *From Plantation to Ghetto* (New York: Hill and Wang, 1976), 25.

3. Ibid., 36.

4. Ibid., 35.

5. William Banks, *The Black Church in the U.S.* (Chicago: Moody Press, 1972), 12–13.

6. Evans, *Are Blacks Spiritually Inferior*, 58.

7. Banks, *Black Church in the U.S.*, 12.

8. E. Franklin Frazier, *The Negro Church in America* (1963; reprint, New York: Schocken Books, 1971), 9–12.

9. W. E. B. Du Bois, *The Negro* (New York: Oxford University Press, 1970).

10. Evans, *Are Blacks Spiritually Inferior*, 52–53.

11. Melville Herskovits, *The Myth of the Negro Past* (Boston: Beacon Press, 1958), 207.

12. Ibid., 47.

13. Evans, *Are Blacks Spiritually Inferior*, 55–56.

14. Ibid., 67.

15. Banks, *Black Church in the U.S.*, 16.

16. Evans, *Are Blacks Spiritually Inferior*, 72–76.

Chapter 2: *The Only Game in Town*

1. Lerone Bennett Jr., *Before the Mayflower*, 5th ed. (New York: Penguin Books, 1961), 214–16.

2. Ibid., 216–17.

3. Ibid., 218.

4. Ibid., 223.

5. Meier and Rudwick, *From Plantation to Ghetto*, 172.

6. Ibid., 173.

7. Bennett, *Before the Mayflower*, 224.

8. Ibid., 225.

9. Ibid., 226.

10. Ibid., 245.

11. Ibid., 246–47.

12. Ibid., 247.

13. The speech was given by Dr. Martin Luther King Jr. during the 1963 March on Washington.

14. Meier and Rudwick, *From Plantation to Ghetto*, 170.

15. Bennett, *Before the Mayflower*, 267–68.

16. C. Eric Lincoln and Lawrence H. Mamiya, *The Black Church in the African American Experience* (Durham, N.C.: Duke University Press, 1990), 196–97.

17. Ibid., 199–202.

18. Ibid., 245–46.

19. Ibid., 251.

Chapter 3: *From Plantation to Ghetto*

1. Meier and Rudwick, *From Plantation to Ghetto*, 195.

2. Ibid., 200.

3. Ibid., 209–10.

4. Leon F. Litwack, *North of Slavery: The Negro in the Free States 1790–1860* (Chicago: University of Chicago Press, 1970), 64.

5. Jawanza Kunjufu, *Countering the Conspiracy to Destroy Black Boys* (Chicago: Kunjufu, 1985), 1.

6. Andrew Hacker, *Two Nations: Black and White, Separate, Hostile, Unequal* (New York: Scribners, 1993), 17–18.

7. Ibid., 18.

8. Lincoln and Mamiya, *The Black Church in the African American Experience*, 247.

9. Meier and Rudwick, *From Plantation to Ghetto*, 221.

10. Bennett, *Before the Mayflower*, 344.

11. Meier and Rudwick, *From Plantation to Ghetto*, 233.

12. Ibid., 233–34.

13. Bennett, *Before the Mayflower*, 344.

14. Ibid.

15. Barbara Carlishe Bigelow, ed., *Contemporary Black Biography*, vol. 5 (Detroit: Gale Research, 1994), 52–57.

16. See Meier and Rudwick, *From Plantation to Ghetto*, 247–48.

17. Meier and Rudwick, *From Plantation to Ghetto*, 253–54.

18. See James Weldon Johnson, *Along This Way* (New York: Penguin Books, 1990), 9.

19. Meier and Rudwick, *From Plantation to Ghetto*, 231.

20. Lincoln and Mamiya, *The Black Church in the African American Experience*, 119.

21. Meier and Rudwick, *From Plantation to Ghetto*, 234.

Chapter 4: *The Rise of Black Denominations*

1. Membership figures and other statistics in this chapter were taken from Robert Famishetti, ed., *The World Almanac and Book of Facts* (Newark: N.J.: Reference Corp., 1996).

2. Lincoln and Mamiya, *The Black Church in the African American Experience*, 27.

3. William L. Banks, *A History of Black Baptists in the United States* (Philadelphia: The Continental Press, 1987), 102.

4. When in 1988 another schism developed over the Boyd family's control of the publishing arm, a new convention of Boyd supporters was formed—the National Missionary Baptist Convention of America.

5. Lincoln and Mamiya, *The Black Church in the African American Experience*, 54.

6. Ibid., 58.

7. Ibid., 60–61.

8. Ibid., 81.

Chapter 5: *The Black Preacher*

1. Henry Mitchell, *Black Preaching* (Philadelphia: Lippincott, 1970), 65.

2. Evans, *Are Blacks Spiritually Inferior*, 95.

3. H. Beecher Hicks, *Images of the Black Preacher* (Valley Forge, Pa.: Judson Press, 1977), 25.

4. Albert J. Raboteau, *Slave Religion* (Oxford: Oxford University Press, 1978), 232.

5. Ibid.

6. Ibid.

7. Isaac Lane, *The Autobiography of Isaac Lane: With a Short History of the C.M.E. Church in America and of Methodism* (Publishing House of the M.E. Church, South, 1916), 52–53.

8. Dwight Perry and Ralph Hammond, "Theological Education of African Americans" (paper presented to the Baptist General Conference Annual Meeting Black Ministries Summit, Estes Park, Colo., June 1992).

9. Booker T. Washington, *Up from Slavery* (New York: Airmont, 1967), 82.

10. See Evans, *Are Blacks Spiritually Inferior*, 112–14.

Chapter 6: *Music in the Black Church*

1. Wyatt Tee Walker, *Somebody's Calling My Name* (Valley Forge, Pa.: Judson Press, 1979), 37.

2. Dearing E. King, "Worship in the Black Church," in *Black Church Life-Styles*, comp. Emmanuel L. McCall (Nashville: Broadman, 1986), 75–76.

3. Milton Sernett, *Afro American Religious History: A Documentary Witness* (Durham, N.C.: Duke University Press, 1985), 110.

4. Wendel Whalum, "Black Hymnody," in *Black Church Life-Styles*, 85.

5. Walker, *Somebody's Calling My Name*, 45–46.

6. Howard Thurman, *International Library of Negro Life and History* (New York: Lindsay Patterson Publishers, 1967).

7. Walker, *Somebody's Calling My Name*, 47.

8. Banks, *Black Church in the U.S.*, 106.

9. Walker, *Somebody's Calling My Name*, 52–59.

10. "Meter," *Compton's Interactive Encyclopedia* (Compton's NewMedia, Inc., 1994).

11. Walker, *Somebody's Calling My Name*, 90.

12. Ibid., 77.

13. Mrs. A. M. Townsend, *The Baptist Standard Hymnal* (Nashville: Sunday School Publishing Board, National Baptist Convention, U.S.A., 1924), 590.

14. Walker, *Somebody's Calling My Name*, 83.

15. Ibid., 97.

16. Ibid., 127.

17. Ibid., 128.

18. Ibid.

19. Ibid., 148.

Chapter 7: Preaching in the Black Church

1. Evans, *Are Blacks Spiritually Inferior*, 102.

2. Mitchell, *Black Preaching*, 65.

3. J. Deotis Roberts, *A Black Political Theology* (Philadelphia: Westminster, 1974), 50.

4. Evans, *Are Blacks Spiritually Inferior*, 103.

5. Henry H. Mitchell, *Black Preaching: The Recovery of a Powerful Art* (Nashville: Abingdon, 1990), 100.

6. See Mitchell, *Black Preaching*, chap. 7.

Chapter 8: From Pulpit to Prison

1. Ralph David Abernathy, *And the Walls Came Tumbling Down* (New York: Harper and Row, 1989), 131–32.

2. Ibid., 132.

3. Ibid., 135–37.

Chapter 9: A New Wave

1. The appendix contains a paper on this concept by Dwight Perry and Ralph Hammond, associate professor of pastoral care at Bethel Seminary, St. Paul, Minnesota, "The Strategic Role of the Black Church" (presented at the annual meeting of the Baptist General Conference, Estes Park, Colo., June 1992).

2. See the documents on racial reconciliation of 1990 and 1995 endorsed jointly by the predominantly White National Association of Evangelicals and the National Black Evangelical Association, representing thousands of churches in America.

3. Joseph Barndt, *Dismantling Racism* (Minneapolis: Augsburg, 1991), 28.

4. Dr. Ruth Bentley, NBEA founding member, interview with author, April 1995.

5. Rev. Russell Knight, president of CURE, interview with author, April 1995.

6. Jerry White, *The Church and the Parachurch: An Uneasy Marriage* (Portland: Multnomah, 1983).

7. Betty Lee Skinner, *Daws: The Story of Dawson Trotman, Founder of the Navigators* (Grand Rapids: Zondervan, 1990).

8. Mark Senter, class notes, "History of Youth Ministry," Trinity Evangelical Divinity School, Deerfield, Ill., fall 1993.

Chapter 11: *Evangelical Ministries in the African American Community*

1. *Carver Bible Institute and College Academic Catalog* (Atlanta, 1994–96), 10.

2. For information on Carver Bible Institute and College, contact Tim Skinner, director of admissions, at 404-527-4520.

3. *Baptist Bible College of Indianapolis Academic Catalog* (Indianapolis, 1994–96), 11.

4. For information on Baptist Bible College of Indianapolis, contact Dr. Charles Ware at 317-352-8736.

5. *Southern Bible Institute Academic Catalog* (Dallas, 1995), 3.

6. For information on Southern Bible Institute, contact Dr. George Mumford at 972-224-5481.

7. For information on Black Light Fellowship, contact Rev. Walter McCray at 128 South Pauline, Chicago, IL 60612 or call 773-556-0081.

8. "History of Urban Ministries Fact Sheet" (Chicago: Urban Ministries Inc., 1995).

9. For information on Urban Ministries Inc., contact Jeff Wright at 1551 Regency Court, Calumet City, IL 60609 or call 708-868-7100.

10. "Company Background Fact Sheet" (Woodbury, N.J.: Renaissance Productions: 1995), 1.

11. Ibid., 4.

12. Ibid., 5.

13. For information on Renaissance Productions, contact Roland Hardy at 537 Mantua Pike, Suite 203, Woodbury, NJ 08096 or call 800-234-2338.

14. For information on Legacy Ministries, contact Dr. Crawford Loritts at 4405 Mall Blvd., Suite 410, Union City, GA 30291 or call 404-969-7278.

15. "Five Year Organizational Plan" (Detroit: Institute of Black Family Development), 1.

16. For information on the Institute of Black Family Development, contact Matthew Parker at 16130 Northland Drive, Southfield, MI 48075.

17. "Background Sheet" (Chicago: CURE, 1995), 2.

18. For information on CURE, contact Rev. Russell Knight at P.O. Box 804113, Chicago, IL 60680-4130 or call 773-374-4330.

19. For information on Urban Evangelical Mission, contact Dr. Ruben Conner at P.O. Box 4939, Dallas, TX 75208 or call 214-565-1912.

20. For information on Lawndale Community Church, contact Rev. Wayne Gordon, 3877 W. Ogden Avenue, Chicago, IL 60623 or call 773-762-0994.

21. For information on Mendenhall Ministries, contact Mendenhall Ministries at 309 Center Street, Mendenhall, MS 39114–3705 or call 601-847-3377.

22. For information on CCDA, contact Wayne Gordon at 3827 W. Ogden Avenue, Chicago, IL 60623 or call 773-762-5772.

23. For information on Circle Urban Ministries, contact Glen Kehrein at 118 N. Central, Chicago, IL 60644 or call 773-921-1466.

24. "Westside Holistic Family Services Information Packet" (Chicago, Ill.: Westside Holistic Family Services, 1995), 1.

25. For information on Westside Holistic Family Services, contact Milicent Lindo at 4909 W. Division Street, Chicago, IL 60651 or call 773-921-8777.

26. For information on *The Alternative*, contact Dr. Tony Evans, at Urban Alternative, 400 Zang Blvd., Dallas, TX 75208 or call 214-943-3868.

27. For information on Glenn Plummer and Associates, contact them at 15565 Northfield Drive, Suite 900, Southfield, MI 48075, or call 248-559-4200.

Bibliography

Abernathy, Ralph David. *And the Walls Came Tumbling Down*. New York: Harper and Row, 1989.

Anyike, James. *Historical Christianity: Africa Centered*. Chicago: Popular Truth, 1994.

Banks, William. *The Black Church in the U.S.* Chicago: Moody Press, 1972.

Barndt, Joseph. *Dismantling Racism*. Minneapolis: Augsburg, 1991.

Bennett, Lerone, Jr. *Before the Mayflower*. Rev. ed. New York: Penguin Books, 1993.

Columbus, Sally, and Ronald Behm. *What Color Is Your God? Black Consciousness and the Christian Faith*. Downers Grove, Ill.: InterVarsity, 1981.

Cone, James H. *Black Theology and Black Power*. New York: The Seabury Press, 1969.

Davidson, Basil. *Africa in History*. New York: Collier Books, 1991.

Du Bois, W. E. B. *Black Reconstruction in America*. New York: Atheneum, 1992.

Evans, Anthony T. *Are Blacks Spiritually Inferior to Whites?: The Dispelling of an American Myth*. Wenonah, N.J.: Renaissance Productions, 1992.

Fisher, Leslie, Jr., and Benjamin Quarles. *The Black American: A Documentary History*. Glenview, Ill.: Scott, Foresman, 1970.

Frazier, E. Franklin. *The Negro Church in America*. Reprint. New York: Schocken Books, 1971.

Gutman, Herbert G. *The Black Family in Slavery and Freedom 1705–1925*. New York: Pantheon, 1976.

Hacker, Andrew. *Two Nations: Black and White, Separate, Hostile, Unequal*. New York: Scribners, 1993.

Haynes, Robert V. *Blacks in White America before 1865*. New York: David McKay, 1972.

Herskovits, Melville J. *The Myth of the Negro Past*. Boston: Beacon Press, 1958.

Johnson, James Weldon. *Along the Way: The Autobiography of James Weldon Johnson*. New York: Viking, 1933.

June, Lee N., ed. *The Black Family: Past, Present and Future*. Grand Rapids: Zondervan, 1991.

Lincoln, C. Eric. *The Black Church since Frazier*. James Gray Lectures given at Duke University, Durham, N.C., 1970.

———. *The Black Experience in Religion*. New York: Anchor, 1974.

Lincoln, C. Eric, and Lawrence H. Mamiya. *The Black Church in the African American Experience*. Durham, N.C.: Duke University Press, 1990.

Litwack, Leon F. *North of Slavery: The Negro in the Free States, 1790–1860*. Chicago: University of Chicago Press, 1970.

McCall, Emmanuel L., comp. *Black Church Life-Styles*. Nashville: Broadman, 1986.

Meier, August, and Elliott Rudwick. *From Plantation to Ghetto*. New York: Hill and Wang, 1976.

Mitchell, Henry H. *Black Preaching*. Philadelphia: Lippincott, 1974.

Mitchell, Henry H. *Black Preaching: The Recovery of a Powerful Art*. Nashville: Abingdon, 1990.

Nelson, Hart M., ed. *The Black Church in America*. New York: Basic Books, 1971.

Patterson, Lindsey, ed. *International Library of Negro Life and History*. New York: Publishers Company, 1967.

Raboteau, Albert J. *Slave Religion*. Oxford: Oxford University Press, 1978.

Roberts, J. Deotis. *A Black Political Theology*. Philadelphia: Westminster, 1974.

Robertson, James Oliver. *American Myth American Reality*. New York: Hill and Wang, 1980.

Sernett, Milton. *Afro American Religious History: A Documentary Witness*. Durham, N.C.: Duke University Press, 1985.

———. *Black Religion and American Evangelicalism*. Metuchen, N.J.: Scarecrow Press, 1975.

Skinner, Betty Lee. *Daws: The Story of Dawson Trotman, Founder of the Navigators*. Grand Rapids: Zondervan, 1990.

Twombly, Robert C. *Blacks in White America since 1865*. New York: David McKay, 1971.

Walker, Wyatt Tee. *Somebody's Calling My Name*. Valley Forge, Pa.: Judson Press, 1979.

Washington, James Melvin. *Conversations with God: Two Centuries of Prayers by African Americans*. New York: Harper Collins, 1994.

Wilmore, Gayrand, and James H. Cover. *Black Theology: A Documentary History, 1966–1979*. Orbis, 1979.

Index

Dwight Perry is professor of pastoral studies at Moody Bible Institute. He has been a pastor, and he has worked with the Baptist General Conference, first as national coordinator of Black ministries and then as associate director of home missions. He has earned a B.A. in history education (with an African American concentration) from the University of Illinois, an M.S. in adult and continuing education from National-Louis University, an M.Ed. in educational psychology from the University of Illinois, and a D.Min. from Covington Theological Seminary. Most recently he earned a Ph.D. in education from Trinity Evangelical Divinity School, in whose M.A. urban ministries program he teaches as an adjunct professor. He is the first African American in the history of Trinity Evangelical Divinity school to earn a Ph.D. degree in any discipline.